PRAISE FOR NOT A TAME LION

An inspiring collection of articles from on
in the UK. It ranges from imaginative p
back from 2023) to deep questioning of cc
There is much food for thought here for practitioners, students and indeed
everyone interested in inner and outer change.

Jocelyn Chaplin, *author of* Deep Equality: Living in the Flow of Natural Rhythms *and* Feminist Counselling in Action

How amazing it is for an 'outsider', a maverick even, to emerge from the margins as the agenda-setter for counselling and psychotherapy. For this is what Nick Totton has done in the past few years! His work on making body therapy relational, on politics and (and in) therapy, on ecopsychology, and on confronting our growth-restricting fears about 'boundaries' is, by now, required reading for all practitioners. I think I learn more from him than from anyone. Those in training or formation should get hold of this provocative, radical and erudite collection. It is where today's excellence in practice lies.

Andrew Samuels, *Professor of Analytical Psychology, University of Essex*

In this volume Totton has brought together 24 of his own papers, including two new papers on professionalisation and regulation, the nature of therapy, therapy in the world, and ecopsychology and embodiment, in a well-organised collection. The central thesis of the book, encapsulated in an eponymous article, is that therapy should not be 'safe' and free of risk; in other words, it is not a tame lion. The main themes and strengths of Totton's work are all here: his detailed knowledge of the history of psychotherapy; his advocacy of the radical origins of therapy, and that the nature of therapy is political and radical; his emphasis on politics as power; his critical analysis of the power of the 'psy' professions and professionalisation; and his keen interest in embodiment and ecology. Readers familiar with Totton's work will be grateful that he has collated and edited his key papers in one volume; readers unfamiliar with his work will find this a rich reader, which includes some personal history and background to Totton's interest in the interplay between psychotherapy and politics. This is a great collection of writings on psychotherapy and politics from a leading exponent in this field who himself is no tame lion, and is essential reading for anyone interested in therapy in its social and political contexts.

Keith Tudor, *Associate Professor at Auckland Institute of Technology, Aotearoa, New Zealand, and Editor of* Psychotherapy and Politics International

Not a Tame Lion

Writings on therapy and its
social and political contexts

Nick Totton

PCCS BOOKS
Ross-on-Wye

PCCS BOOKS
2 Cropper Row
Alton Road
Ross-on-Wye
HR9 5LA
UK
Tel +44 (0)1989 763900
www.pccs-books.co.uk

First published 2012

This collection © Nick Totton, 2012

All rights reserved.

No part of this publication may be reproduced, stored in a retrieval system, transmitted or utilised in any form by any means, electronic, mechanical, photocopying or recording or otherwise without permission in writing from the publishers.

Nick Totton has asserted his rights to be identified as the author of this work in accordance with the Copyright, Designs and Patents Act 1988.

Not a Tame Lion: Writings on therapy and its social and political contexts

ISBN 978 1 906254 48 3

Cover artwork 'Indian Yellow' by Hélène Fletcher
Cover designed in the UK by Old Dog Graphics
Typeset in the UK by The Old Dog's Missus in 'Univers'
Printed in the UK by ImprintDigital, Exeter

Contents

Acknowledgements		v
Introduction		vii
Part 1: Professionalisation and Regulation		**1**
1	The Baby and the Bathwater: 'Professionalisation' in psychotherapy and counselling	3
2	Munching Through the Rainforest: Expertise and its resistance	15
3	Looking Back	20
4	The Defeat of State Regulation in the UK	22
Part 2: The Nature of Therapy		**27**
5	The Battle for Reality	29
6	Two Ways of Being Helpful	33
7	Depending on Each Other	38
8	'Intimacy Took Place'	44
9	An Extraordinary Ordinariness	51
10	Both/And	60
11	Boundaries and Boundlessness	63
12	Not a Tame Lion: Psychotherapy in a safety-obsessed culture	71
Part 3: Therapy in the World		**83**
13	Upstream Runners and Instream Waders	85
14	*Psychotherapy and Politics International*: First editorial	88
15	Psychotherapy and Politics: Is there an alternative?	91

16	Can Psychotherapy Help Make a Better Future?	96
17	Democracy and Therapy	110
18	In and Out of the Mainstream: Therapy in its social and political context	115
19	May '68	128
20	Editing *The Politics of Psychotherapy*	132

Part 4: Ecopsychology and Embodiment — 139

21	Embodied Relating	141
22	Overwhelm	150
23	Wild Therapy	152
24	The Body in the World, the World in the Body	157
	References	165
	Index	177

ACKNOWLEDGEMENTS

Most of these pieces have appeared in earlier versions in the following publications; thanks are due to the editors and publishers.

Chapter 1: The baby and the bathwater: 'Professionalisation' in psychotherapy and counselling. *British Journal of Guidance and Counselling*, *27*(3), 1999, pp 313-24.

Chapter 2: Munching through the rainforest: Expertise and its resistance. *European Journal of Psychotherapy and Counselling*, *8*(4), 2006, pp 423-7.

Chapter 3: Editorial, *Psychotherapy and Politics International*, *6*(3), 2008, pp 155-6.

Chapter 4: *The Script*, *42*(1), 2012, pp 1-3.

Chapter 5: Power in the therapy room. *Therapy Today*, *20*(7), 2009, 16-19.

Chapter 6: Two ways of being helpful. *CPJ*, *15*(10), 2004, pp 5-8.

Chapter 7: In defence of dependency. *Therapy Today*, *17*(5), 2006, pp 18-21.

Chapter 9: An extraordinary ordinariness. *European Journal of Psychotherapy and Counselling*, *13*(1), 2011, pp 69-75.

Chapter 11: Boundaries and boundlessness. *Therapy Today*, *21*(8), 2010, pp 11-15.

Chapter 12: Not a tame lion: Psychotherapy in a safety-obsessed culture. In L Bondi, D Carr, C Clark & C Clegg (Eds), *Towards Professional Wisdom* (pp 233-46). Ashgate Publishing, 2011.

Chapter 13: From the Introduction (pp xiii-xv) of *The Politics of Psychotherapy*, N Totton (Ed), Open University Press, 2006.

Chapter 14: *Psychotherapy and Politics International*, *1*(1), 2003, pp iii-iv.

Chapter 15: Psychotherapy and politics: Is there an alternative? *Group-Analytic Contexts*, *54*, 2011, pp 17-21.

Chapter 16: Can psychotherapy help make a better future? *Psychotherapy and Politics International*, *3*(2), 2005, pp 83-95.

Chapter 17: Democracy and therapy. *Therapy Today*, *18*(1), 2007, pp 7-10.

Chapter 18: In and out of the mainstream: Therapy in its social and political context. In S Haugh & S Paul (Eds), *The Therapeutic Relationship* (pp 145-55). PCCS Books, 2008.

Chapter 19: Two editorials from *Psychotherapy and Politics International*, *6*(2), 2008, pp 73-4 and *8*(3), 2010, pp 179-80.

Chapter 20: Editing *The Politics of Psychotherapy*. *Psychotherapy and Politics International*, *6*(2), 2008, pp 82-90.

Chapter 22: Overwhelm. *Psychotherapy and Politics International*, *8*(2), 2010, pp 93-5.

Chapter 23: Wild therapy. *Therapy Today*, *22*(2), 2011, pp 10-14.

Chapter 24: The body in the world, the world in the body. *Therapy Today*, *23*(3), 2012, pp 20-3.

For my dear partner Hélène Fletcher,
who shares my passion in these matters

Introduction

And because they are humane, and concerned, and even love us, and are very frightened, they will try to cure us. They may succeed. But there is still hope that they will fail.

(RD Laing)

When the idea came to me of assembling various articles and chapters into a book, I thought I might possibly have 20,000 words, enough for a slim volume. There turned out to be over 100,000 words to choose from; and after eliminating redundancies and culling material not worth reprinting, I have come up with this reasonably sizeable collection of 60,000-plus words covering about 15 years (during which time I have also written or edited 15 books). In case you wonder, I'm not sure where I found the time.

In what follows I have concentrated on a topic which is central to my interests: therapy in its social and political contexts – interpreted in quite a generous sense. (And by the way, 'therapy' here and throughout the book indicates psychotherapy and counselling.) This has meant that, for example, I have not included more technical writings on body psychotherapy (what I do for a living, and as a passion); but I have included some general pieces arguing for the importance of body psychotherapy as a modality, and exploring its social and political significance. I have included not only writings about the relationship between therapy and society as a whole, but also writings about the internal politics of the field, and discussions of how the practice of therapy, so far as I am concerned, has social and political implications – in both directions: for instance, if, as I argue in Chapter 12, therapy is intrinsically without goals, this means that it is inappropriate to harness it to the task of relieving symptoms and getting people back to work; but it also means that therapy offers a model for a different, Taoist–anarchist kind of politics, based not on policies and demands but on process – such as we see in the Occupy movement, and which I explore more fully in my recent book *Wild Therapy* (Totton, 2011c).

Quite a lot of the material collected here was also used in creating *Wild Therapy*; and I think (hope) it will be interesting for readers of that book to see where and how its ideas developed, over a period of more than a decade. I have tried to eliminate a good deal of repetition; but sometimes I have left bits in because to remove them would have made my argument incomprehensible, and sometimes I have left them in because saying the same thing from different angles and in different contexts can enrich its meaning. This is one advantage of a collection over a unified book, and I didn't want to waste it.

It has actually been fascinating and surprising to notice my favourite riffs recurring, and to think about why I have become so attached to these particular thoughts. Some key examples are the concept of local knowledge, and its polarisation with expert systems; the analogy of pidgin and creole as a way of thinking about the therapeutic relationship; Denis Postle's characterisation of therapy as a rainforest rather than a monoculture; the insistence that therapy is always political because it always involves a notion of how people should be; the suggestion that therapy should be, in part, a conscious power struggle; and the image of the Therapy Police.

Each of these ideas, it seems to me, illuminates an aspect of my overall concern, which is in a sense, oddly enough, a historical one: at this point in time therapy seems in danger of forgetting where it came from, and hence what it is about. This is something we are very used to seeing in our clients: they often come, consciously or otherwise, because they have lost their history, and need to recover it. But therapy itself, as a culture, is bizarrely bad at remembering its own history: if you ask most practitioners they will have a very vague idea even about how their own modality developed, and almost none beyond that – including how and why their modality separated itself out from the field: they will be familiar with the modality's internal creation myth – 'our founder sprung fully formed from a couch, he (usually he) was persecuted by envious peers but finally triumphed' – but generally not with how the story looks from the outside.

This collective amnesia makes it hard to understand ourselves as a cultural phenomenon; and hard or impossible to see the repeated patterns which tell us so much about the politics of therapy. An example which I mention more than once in this collection is the way in which in the early 1950s – the first stages of therapy's previous era of conservatism – trainers complained about the arrival on the scene of would-be practitioners who were essentially 'normal', but not in a good way: candidates who were conventional in their personal style and untroubled by the shadow side of mainstream culture, and who saw therapy as a way of getting ahead in the world. This tension between an 'old guard' who see themselves as rebels at odds with current social arrangements, and new trainees who take it for granted that therapy is a part of the mainstream rather than a critique of it, is repeating in the present day.

I think the deeper problem which fuels this repetition is that therapy has always accepted the Western cultural paradigm of 'individual versus group'. Sometimes it supports the collective, and encourages the individual to adapt to it and become 'well-adjusted' (Totton, 2000: 96–7, 106–7); sometimes it encourages the individual to rebel and seek her so-called 'real self' (Geller, 1982). Each position is one-sided, and each is based on the assumption that individual and group are opposed. Ecological ways of seeing, however – matching the viewpoints of many non-Western cultures – encourage us to understand that individual and group are complementary, even co-created (Macy, 1991; Totton, 2011c: 28–30). The individual cannot exist or be understood without the systems of which it is part; likewise, the system cannot exist or be understood without the individuals who make it up. We each – as client or as practitioner – bring our entire relational context into the therapy room with us; in a sense, it is between these two systems that therapy takes place, the two individuals concerned being only their representatives.

As I say, this is an ecological viewpoint; and I have included a couple of pieces on ecopsychology, which is currently central to my way of thinking about therapy. My hope is to contribute to a process which, rather than bolting the outside and the wild on to ordinary therapeutic practice, completely reconceives psychotherapy in line with ecological perceptions. The furthest development so far of this project has been in my chapter in *Vital Signs* (Totton, 2012). Putting individuals back into their context – what I call in Chapter 24 of the book 'discovering the social in the individual' – is one aspect of ecologically informed therapy; another aspect, and a theme which has been important to me for a long time, is relativism.

As I argue in Chapter 16, this volume, therapy is a practice of truth; by which I mean not that it claims to reveal an absolute truth – just the opposite, that through the ways in which it interrogates our perceptions and beliefs it helps us to see that absolute truth *does not exist*, and that everything depends on where we are standing. In my view this is the great discovery of modernity, potentially liberating us from fundamentalism and essentialism of all kinds. Far from being, as some people experience relativism, a negative assertion that there is no truth, it discovers truth everywhere – truth not singular but plural and contingent, and therefore subject to negotiation.

It would be absurd to take this position without acknowledging that it, too, is *my* truth rather than *the* truth; as is everything that I find in therapy, both what I like and what I react against. For me, therapy is inherently anarchistic in its thrust, deconstructing dogma and hierarchy and supporting personal empowerment and responsibility. But then, not coincidentally, I am an anarchist myself, and was one before I encountered therapy. Like everyone else, I construct my own therapy from the bits I like out of a much larger picture. I hope that readers find interest and value in my personal mosaic.

Before I leave you to the book, though – or leave the book to you – I want to say something about its title. As many will recognise, it comes from *The Lion, the Witch and the Wardrobe*; the full passage appears as the epigraph to Chapter 12. It seems to me an excellent antidote to the rather insipid over-emphasis on safety which dominates current conventional thinking about therapy. As CS Lewis says of Aslan, he's not *safe*; but he's *good*. I would say the same of therapy: that by its nature, it always includes an element of risk, not as an unfortunate side effect, but as something essential to its functioning: it is unsafe in the way that entering into any intimate relationship is unsafe.

Safety and risk function as two polarities within the therapeutic space: both are required to create a charge of energy. A fuller picture, in fact, might have this polarity crossed at right angles with another one, between excitement and relaxation: again, both are required, and if the therapeutic encounter moves too far in any direction from the centre the energy field will collapse, and nothing useful will happen.

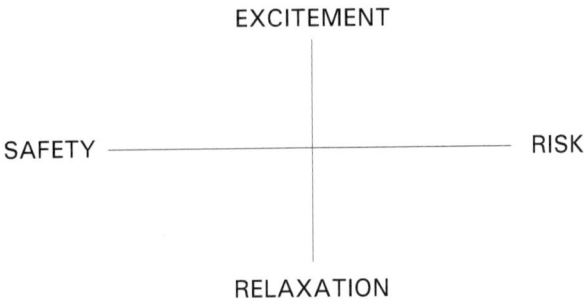

Poles of the therapeutic field

In many ways, this introduction serves to re-emphasise why I have opposed state regulation of psychotherapy and counselling so strongly and for so long. Therapy in the service of the state's goals, and subject to its dreadful regime of risk-averse normalisation and surveillance, cannot function in the ways which for me carry its value – as a constant testing and questioning of our assumptions, certainly about the world and other people, but most centrally about ourselves. When in Chapter 4 I speak of 'the defeat of state regulation in the UK', it is a (strategic) overstatement. State regulation has been taken off the immediate agenda; but it has not been permanently stopped. Those who believe they would benefit from regulation, or who simply hate the sorts of ideas which stopped it in its tracks, have not gone away; they are regrouping. So this collection of direct or implicit arguments about the wild nature of therapy, and its intrinsic unsuitability for domestication, seem to me well worth assembling.

Part 1
Professionalisation and Regulation

1

The Baby and the Bathwater: 'Professionalisation' in psychotherapy and counselling

> I have slowly come to the conclusion that if we did away with 'the expert', 'the certified professional', 'the licensed psychologist', we might open our profession to a breeze of fresh air, a surge of creativity, such as has not been known for years. In every area – medicine, nursing, teaching, bricklaying, or carpentry – certification has tended to freeze and narrow the profession, has tied it to the past, has discouraged innovation. ... The question I am humbly raising, in the face of what I am sure will be great shock and antagonism, is simply this: Can psychology find a new and better way?
> (Rogers, 1973/1980: 246–7)

The rush to professionalisation

> Good morning, lemmings
> (Railway graffiti near Paddington Station, London)

The unfortunate truth is that the primary response to Carl Rogers' question, in 1973 and now, is not so much 'shock and antagonism' as a deafening silence. Rogers (who developed the term 'counselling' because he was himself unable to get certified as a psychotherapist) is by no means the first significant figure in the field to oppose aspects of professionalisation – for example Freud (1926a) vehemently objected to the medical model of psychoanalysis which was intimately tied to professionalisation (R Jacoby, 1986: 145), while Jung said of psychotherapy that 'holding lectures, giving instruction, pumping in knowledge, all these ... procedures are of no use here' (Jung, 1976: 534).

Many eminent and well-respected contemporary figures have also expressed reactions ranging from horror to despair at what is

---

1999. Probably my first academic publication, in the *British Journal of Guidance and Counselling*, by invitation of Colin Feltham. One referee hated it, one liked it; Colin used his casting vote. The article is in some ways a historical relic, but in other ways still surprisingly relevant. It is also the first outing for my favourite theme of expert versus local knowledge.

happening to counselling and psychotherapy, both in the UK and in the USA (e.g. Heron, 1990/2011; Lomas, 1997/2011; O'Hara, 1997; Thorne, 1995/2011). The opponents of headlong professionalisation have largely dominated the argument; but its proponents' strategy of what in German is called *Totschweigen* (deathly silence), combined with remorseless organisational advance, meets with continued success.

What is 'headlong professionalisation'? This question can readily be answered by scanning the pages of just about any recent issue of a trade journal in the field. For example, the August 1998 issue of *Counselling*, the journal of the British Association for Counselling (BAC), includes a letter from David Buckingham which says:

> Counsellor training is still expanding. There are ten times as many diploma courses as there were a few years ago. The cart appears to be before the horse. Courses are offered, places are filled, and there is a hope that there will be enough available clients to provide the practice the students require. ... [H]ow long will it be before placements and clients realise that they are onto a good thing, and begin to charge us for the privilege of counselling them?
> (Buckingham, 1998: 175)

There are also several letters both for and against the new BAC accreditation requirement of 40 hours of personal therapy or counselling. Those in favour mainly focus on what Richards, Hargaden and Beazley Richards (1998: 173) call 'the need for practitioners to be engaged in a constant process of self examination, especially in the way they relate to others'. The arguments against are mainly either that research has not demonstrated the value of personal therapy in training effective practitioners; or simply that personal therapy is too hard, too unpredictable and too expensive!

Two other pieces from the same issue stand out as relevant. In the *Point of View* section, Sally Saunders argues that:

> If counselling trainings are financially directed, they will be consumer-led. The consumers ... may understandably choose a course that does not have the demand for personal therapy because it is cheaper to train. ... If counselling training was seen more as an apprenticeship allowing students to develop at their own pace, it might stop the rush for hasty qualification and the pressure to know it all now. ... It is surely time to re-evaluate what counselling is and who should be doing it.
> (Saunders, 1998: 179–80)

And in an interview entitled 'Counselling and the abuse of power', Ernesto Spinelli, Academic Dean of the School of Psychotherapy and Counselling at Regent's College, London, questions the introduction of new standards of professionalisation through endless working parties, committees and guidelines:

> [A]ll of these things give an illusion of professional bodies. We say: 'Look, if we go to all of these meetings, if we have all these standards, if we have these codes of ethics, we must be professionals.' And we can hide our questions, about what we are professionals *of*, or *in*, or *about*, by having all these bodies to protect us.
>
> (Spinelli, 1998: 182)

I am quoting these various viewpoints to establish the ferment of confusion, doubt and disagreement which currently pervades the field – and through which the professionalisers continue to carve their determined single track.

To speak bluntly, counselling and psychotherapy training in the UK is close to being a bubble: a pyramid selling scheme, in which individuals or organisations near the top of the food chain skim off large profits, and those near the bottom starve or eat each other. Far more practitioners are being trained than there are clients available for them; and a series of emergency measures are being used to stave off the collapse of the system by lengthening the food chain further, inserting more roles and jobs – as well as client and therapist, we now have trainer, supervisor, trainer's supervisor, supervisor's trainer, supervisor's trainer's supervisor – as Spinelli 'sometimes jokingly says' to students and trainees, 'we'll eventually reach a point where we'll no longer need clients, because we can just close the circle, we can counsel each other, supervise each other, and train each other ... ad infinitum' (Spinelli, 1998: 183).

If only this were the case! But unfortunately a supply of clients must be generated, at approximately 15 or 20 times the rate at which practitioners are being turned out (assuming that a full practice has 15 or 20 slots). The best hope for achieving this is to colonise the public sphere of free-to-the-client therapy. But as with pyramid schemes, collapse is inevitable – far sooner, usually, than the participants anticipate. Perhaps we should go back to Sally Saunders' questions quoted above: what are counselling and psychotherapy, and who should be doing them?

Deep background

> Slowly but surely psychoanalysis was cleansed of all Freud's achievements. Bringing psychoanalysis into line with the world, which shortly before had threatened to annihilate it, took place inconspicuously at first. ... Form eclipsed content; the organisation became more important than its task.
> (Reich, 1942/1973: 125)

All this has happened before. In his 1954 paper 'Therapeutic problems in the analysis of the "normal" candidate', the American psychoanalyst Maxwell Gitelson reports that some analysts 'have begun to despair of the suitability of "normal" candidates for a career in psycho-analysis' (Gitelson, 1954/1989: 413). He quotes Hans Eissler, who, after working with someone who wanted therapy 'only for professional reasons', decided that he 'would never again try the analysis of a "normal" person' (p. 414). Gitelson also quotes the then President of the American Psychoanalytic Association, Robert Knight, on how 'the great increase in numbers of trainees ... and ... the more structured training of institutes' had changed the sort of people coming for training. In the 1920s and early 1930s, Knight says,

> many gifted individuals with definite neuroses or character disorders were trained. They were primarily introspective individuals, inclined to be studious and thoughtful, and tended to be highly individualistic ... read prodigiously and knew the psycho-analytic literature thoroughly ...
> In contrast, perhaps the majority of students of the past decade or so have been 'normal' characters, or perhaps one should say had 'normal character disorders'. They are not introspective, are inclined to read only the literature that is assigned in institute courses, and wish to get through with the training requirements as rapidly as possible. ... Their motivation for being analysed is more to get through this requirement of training rather than to ... explore introspectively and with curiosity their own inner selves. ... The partial capitulation of some institutes arising from numbers of students, from their ambitious haste, and from their tendency to be satisfied with a more superficial grasp of theory, has created some of the training problems we now face.
> (Knight, 1953: 217–18)

There is an uncanny parallel with some of the passages from *Counselling*. The same complaint is being made that people are training for the wrong reasons, coming from the wrong place internally, that they are concerned with the job rather than the work, and with looking into others rather than into themselves; and for the same underlying reasons – like American psychoanalysis in the 1950s, the occupation of psychotherapy and counselling has shifted to a more central and acceptable cultural position.

The rise of the 'normal' practitioner dovetails very neatly with the re-medicalisation of therapy. People have struggled for decades to establish that psychotherapy is, as Freud said of psychoanalysis, 'not a specialised branch of medicine' (Freud, 1926a: 252); that those wanting therapy are not *sick*, since unhappiness or a desire to change are not illnesses. The drive to professionalisation, the enormous expansion of training, demands a huge increase in clients. The only way to get enough therapy and counselling paid for, it appears, is to get the state and other institutions to pay for it. For this to happen, psychotherapy and counselling must present themselves as somehow *medical*.

In the United States, the dominant issue has been getting therapy paid for by medical insurance. Reasonably enough from their point of view, the insurers have required that the treatment they are paying for is medical treatment: in other words, that the client is defined as ill. A whole profession of 'managed care' has arisen to administer this process; demanding that each client is assigned a 'DSM number' – a psychiatric definition, based on the *Diagnostic and Statistical Manual of Mental Disorders,* fourth edition (*DSM-IV*) (American Psychiatric Association, 1994), of the supposed disease entity from which they are suffering. (The diagnostic categories of *DSM-IV* are a masterpiece of circularity and vacuity; for example '312.9: Disruptive Behavior Disorder', the primary sign of which is disruptive behaviour.) Each DSM number is allotted a fixed number of authorisable sessions, irrespective of the individual client's needs.

Internet users will be familiar with expressions of outrage from American practitioners over the distortions of therapeutic relationship and process entailed. (For a print account, see e.g. O'Hara, 1997: 24–8; also Totton 1997/2011a: 129–30.) We in the UK may congratulate ourselves on having escaped. But we have our own mild-mannered version of managed care: the presence of counselling and psychotherapy in the National *Health* Service, which, although it lets therapy reach large numbers of people who would not otherwise get it (although they may not always want it or be suitable for it), also means that the concept of audited, cost-effective, time-limited therapy and counselling becomes central (House, 1996; Totton, 1997/2011a). And, of course, the NHS benefits in turn from the training bubble by being able frequently to pay GP practice counsellors a pittance – it is a buyer's market.

Expert systems/local knowledges

> I have felt for some years now like a man who is in danger because he has become imprisoned in the profession of therapy.
> (Thorne, 1995/2011: 161)

The sociology of professions emphasises two defining features of a profession: the possession of 'expert knowledge' (Giddens, 1991; Stehr, 1994), and the use of political strategies to establish a small elite group in control of its own boundaries. These strategies include 'social closure' (Parkin, 1974), 'occupational imperialism' (Larkin, 1983), state support and market control (Larson, 1977). The medical profession can serve as a template of such processes, and a number of authors have described its use of such strategies to establish a uniquely powerful role for itself (e.g. Cant & Sharma, 1996; Griggs, 1982; Larkin, 1983; Stacey, 1992).

Psychotherapy and counselling – or rather, powerful groups within these occupations – are trying in many ways to repeat the success of medicine. This is partly in resistance to medicine's 'occupational imperialism': one of the powerful forces in the development of the Rugby Conference, which ultimately became the United Kingdom Council for Psychotherapy (UKCP), was the fear that psychiatry would attempt to 'own' the activity of psychotherapy, as it does in many European countries (Heron, 1990; Wasdell, 1992/2011).

Psychotherapy and counselling have responded to the political need for a body of 'expert knowledge' by generating one – radically lengthening and widening trainings, 'technicalising' every aspect of the work, inserting new levels and meta-levels of expertise and qualification. All this in a field where research finds repeatedly that *technique and outcome cannot be shown to be connected*, that '[t]here are ... hundreds of different versions of psychotherapy, and many of them seem to work equally well' (Mair, 1992: 146).

This verdict (backed up by, for instance, Orlinsky and Howard, 1986, and Frank, 1973) seems to, but doesn't, support the notion of *generic* therapy, which is vital to any notion of expert knowledge: the idea that everyone is in some sense doing the same thing. There are hundreds of different forms of marriage in the world, many of which seem to work equally well; but they are not all the same thing. And what do we mean, anyway, by 'work', in the context of a complex relationship like marriage or therapy? The UKCP, especially, finds itself in the position of gathering together under one roof people whose activities have virtually no point of similarity with one another. (Stacey, 1994: 110, sees a parallel situation in medicine.) The rationale is the creation of a generic profession, but it appears that any non-empty definition of what that profession *does* leaves out half of its supposed practitioners.

Many people have expressed unease on every level at this process, but it has often been difficult to produce a clear critique of the notion of expertise. A helpful concept here is that of *local knowledge* (Geertz, 1983): a term developed in anthropology and the new field of science studies to describe the opposite pole from generalised expertise which is:

> formulated on a global level, that is, within the abstract 'synthetic nature' constructed by science. And the terms it is built on are to be highly standardized, quantifiable and not subject to subjective interpretations. It is through such a model, its language and its terms that the necessary control, manipulation and supervision ... is established.
> (Van der Ploeg, 1993: 219)

Van der Ploeg's seminal paper 'Potatoes and knowledge' (1993) studies the interplay between agrarian science and local farmers in the Andes. It describes how, from the scientists' point of view, it is 'only logical' to model the needs and procedures of agriculture in a standardised way, with so much nitrogen required equalling such and such a dose of chemical fertiliser, and so on. The practical reality of farming, for someone who knows the intricacies of their environment and works by what van der Ploeg calls *'art de la localité'*, is very different. 'However, the outcome of such methods cannot be exactly predicted. Nor can the necessary methods ... be prescribed in detail. ... Local knowledge ... is, under these conditions, rapidly becoming not just a marginal, but more than anything, a superfluous or even a counter-productive element' (van der Ploeg, 1993: 219–20).

A closely similar struggle between expert systems and local knowledge is being played out within the field of psychotherapy and counselling. Brian Wynne characterises local knowledges – which are always necessarily plural – as:

> interwoven with *practices* ... highly dynamic systems of knowledge involving continuous negotiation between 'mental'

and 'manual' [for our purposes, practical] labour, and continual interpretation of production experiences. ... However because it is so multidimensional and adaptive, experience is rarely expressed in a univocal, clear form. This is frequently mistaken for lack of theoretical content ... [But] there is indeed systematic theory, even though this is in a syntax linked to the local labour process and does not presuppose a universal and impersonal world.

(Wynne, 1995: 67, italics added)

Is this not an excellent description of the 'knowledge system' of psychotherapy and counselling – 'multidimensional and adaptive', 'interwoven with practices'? The concept of local knowledge helps to clarify and support the repeated protests of figures like Peter Lomas (e.g. 1987, 1974/1994) that psychotherapy is a matter of experience, intuition and human sensitivity – wisdom, in fact – rather than of technique and expertise; or Jung's statement that 'any organisation that proposes collective methods seems to me unsuitable, because it would be sawing off the branch on which the psychotherapist sits' (Jung, 1976: 534). It underlines the crucial role of self-knowledge (the self being a large part of the *localité* for this particular art), and the real appropriateness of the apprenticeship model.

We can now clarify the quite straightforward socio-politico-economic reasons why counselling and psychotherapy appear to be turning their backs on their own hard-won local knowledges. *A profession must have its expertise* – which must articulate with the hegemonic expertise of its society. This expertise:

would have key characteristics: it would be taught in an organized way, most usually in a university (or at least in an institution that collects, transmits and eventually reproduces knowledge); and it would be standardized and accredited and often have scientific anchorage. ... Expert knowledge gives some the privilege to speak, to act as arbiters.

(Cant & Sharma, 1996: 6)

It is no accident that the expert systems/local knowledges dichotomy is explicitly linked with themes of colonialism and imperialism. Generic psychotherapy and counselling have used a specious version of expert knowledge to colonise and weld into an empire many diverse local craft knowledges – hence distorting them, much as medical chemistry isolates a supposed 'active ingredient' from a medicinal plant (Griggs, 1982). The political impetus is so strong that it has managed to ignore how 'scientific research' itself – the system's own borrowed expertise – finds repeatedly that, although therapy and counselling seem generally beneficial, *neither technique nor training significantly affect the benefits reported* (House, 1997/2011, Mair, 1992, and Mowbray, 1995, all offer surveys of relevant research; for a particularly interesting example see Seligman, 1995). What *does* make therapy effective is precisely 'local knowledge' – the 'therapeutic bond' and all the imponderables on which it depends. [Author note: It is now clear that even more important to outcome than the therapeutic relationship are the psychological and social resources of individual clients entering therapy: Cooper, 2008, 60*ff*.]

Another closely related metaphor has been used by Postle (1997/2011, 1998), drawing on Shiva's (1993) concept of 'monocultures of the mind'. Like the multinational companies, generic psychotherapy and counselling extinguish local ecosystems in the interest of economies of uniformity, 'weeding out' the unique and nonconformist. As Postle points out, 'a register [of acceptable practitioners] *creates* weeds. Indeed for it to make sense, it *has* to create weeds, to justify the high cost of the education of cultivars' (Postle, 1998: 154).

The close parallel between what is happening in psychotherapy and counselling, and the historical, global effect of Western science and capitalism on local knowledge systems, is made eloquently clear in Maureen O'Hara's account of the current American situation:

> Managed care spokespeople openly describe their revolution as the industrialization of health care and, with unconcealed enthusiasm and frequently contempt, declare that the days of 'therapy as a cottage industry' are over. What is happening to therapists in the 1990s is equated with what happened to butchers, bakers and candlestick-makers in the 1800s.
> (O'Hara, 1997: 24)

The good of the client

> The opinion of the United Kingdom Council for Psychotherapy seems to be that a recognised training is required in order for psychotherapists to be effective. There does not appear to be much evidence to support this opinion.
> (Mair, 1992: 150)

Professionalisation has its own self-motivating dynamic: once a group decides to carve out a niche as a profession, it inevitably seeks to make boundaries around itself and to control admission.

Perhaps the only way to achieve this is by laying claim to a body of expert knowledge. The fundamental motivation involved is quite simply one of self-interest. However, like many social phenomena (Levi-Strauss, 1967), the drive to professionalisation is not conscious of its own dynamic: it holds false beliefs about its own motivations. The primary conscious belief is that professionalisation is *for the good of the client*: that it will protect the public from being preyed upon by dangerous, incompetent and unscrupulous quacks.

Unfortunately there is practically no evidence in support of this belief, and a good deal against it. Richard Mowbray (1995) has extensively documented the practical, philosophical and technical reasons for doubting that registration or licensing protects the client; he draws on a wide range of sources, including Hogan's magisterial four volume work (1979). We can conclude the same thing from the everyday evidence of abusive behaviour in the long-regulated medical and legal professions (Stacey, 1992, 1994). What is more, every experienced practitioner knows that practitioner abuse occurs in the most respectable and senior areas of the field, not just on the wild fringes. One well-documented example is the past president of the American Psychiatric Association and the American Psychoanalytic Association, and honorary life president of the World Association for Social Psychiatry, who was found to have raped patients whom he injected with amytal (Noel & Watterson, 1992).

At least as bad as the false reassurance of expertise, wisdom and unimpeachability is the standardised 'complaints procedure' based upon an adversarial, quasi-legal structure quite inappropriate to the sorts of situations which arise in psychotherapy and counselling (Totton, 1997/2011b). Grinding on for month after month, fitting the client to the structure rather than the structure to the client, and finally producing at best a largely irrelevant verdict of 'guilty' or 'not guilty', complaints procedures are often disastrous for all involved. Most differences between practitioner and client are far better suited to a conflict resolution model than to a legal one. What unhappy clients often want more than anything is an apology, an acknowledgement of hurt; and, of course, this is the one thing that the professionalised complaints procedure prevents them from having. In what Brian Thorne has called 'this death-dealing culture of accountability and appraisal where the basic assumption is that nobody is really trustworthy' (Thorne, 1995/2011: 167), few practitioners will dare acknowledge error, for fear of being hung, drawn and quartered *pour encourager les autres*.

The most striking aspect of all this is the extraordinary way in which practitioners have amputated their own understanding of human psychological processes. We know about the projection of shadow figures; yet we go on talking about all these dangerous abusive therapists 'out there', and setting up ways to hound and expel scapegoats – as if this will somehow resolve our own feelings of resentment and even hatred towards our clients, for stirring us up in so many painful ways (Winnicott, 1947/1987). And accompanying this hatred, there is perhaps a profound *fear* of our clients and how they may treat us.

The professionalisation process can be understood as one of *expulsion*. Something is being got rid of; for overdetermined motives, including the formation of boundaries towards 'social closure', and the inculcation of public anxiety about who is a 'safe' therapist. But the motivations also include, it seems, a fantasy that we can get rid of all the messy, dirty, chaotic aspects of therapy and counselling – 'cut back' the weeds, the 'sprawling plants' that 'obscure each other's light and deprive each other of nutrients' (van Deurzen, 1996; see Postle, 1998). This powerful and alarming metaphor, in an address by a former chair of UKCP, raises Kleinian spectres of infantile envy and hatred, closely parallel to the suggestion that we may be throwing out the baby with the dirty bathwater which we would so much like to deny. But the dirtiness is intrinsic to the baby; and the baby is what we will, as therapists and counsellors, always be left holding.

'There is no alternative'

> Where, I ask, is the soul in all this? Could it be that all the energy I have devoted over the years to schemes for accreditation and recognition, all the many hours spent in committees and in working parties ... instead of improving the quality of therapy and enhancing the well-being of both therapists and clients has led instead to the creation of an exclusive professionalism and added anxiety, competitiveness and the fear of judgement to the lives of those who were previously lovingly and conscientiously responding to the needs of their clients?
>
> (Thorne, 1995/2011: 167)

The proponents of professionalisation have so far lost the argument – partly because they have chosen not to join it. Unfortunately, though, arguments are not everything; tremendously powerful forces are involved. At bottom, psychotherapy and counselling are reflecting the values of capitalist society at the end of the twentieth century: standardisation, form over content, 'give the customer what they want (and never tell them about other possibilities)'. The one argument to which professionalisers return again and again is a sad but effective one: it's bound to happen. There is no alternative.

This is not wholly the case. Certainly there is and will continue to be 'professionalised' psychotherapy and counselling: hierarchical, consumer-driven and shored up by an easy scientistic posture of expertise. It seems likely, though, that other forms of practice and organisation will in fact survive, and even flourish. As Foucault tells us (e.g. Foucault: 1980), power and resistance are inseparable: every form of control and centralisation immediately creates an uncontrollable margin. Many practitioners from all schools have revolted against professionalisation, because it so directly flouts all their 'local knowledge' – what they have learnt *in practice* about the interactions which are central to their craft; and because it means organising collectively in a way which actively contradicts their skilled understanding of human nature and human groups. Some are already grouping together to do something else: at least one organisation, the Independent Practitioners Network, is striving to create forms of accreditation and validation which emerge from, rather than flout, therapeutic practice – in this case, based on a network of peer groups (Totton, 1998a, Chapter 2, this volume).

It is inappropriate to take some sort of Luddite stance, mourning the loss of the Good Old Days: they were never that good, in our field or any other. Local knowledges have traditionally been hamstrung by lack of meta-perspective, of the understanding that they are in fact *local* knowledges; without this awareness they become dogmas and rituals, preventing the development of new and better ways. The professionalisation debate has, not always intentionally, cast a great deal of light on hitherto 'unconscious' aspects of our work – including aspects, like lack of accountability, that urgently need changing. We cannot go back to the past. The issue is about the future: and the future of psychotherapy and counselling, just like the future of our society in general, is still in contest.

2

Munching Through the Rainforest: Expertise and its resistance

It is a fundamental fallacy to believe that it is possible by the elaboration of machinery to escape the necessity of trusting one's fellow human beings.
(Clement Attlee)

As I hope readers will already know, each year vast swathes of the Amazon rainforest are stripped bare – primarily for industrial-scale monoculture of soya beans, which will be eaten by cattle. After a few years of this, the thin soil is no longer useful for anything; the rainforest, which is the richest and most complex environment on the planet, full of unique species, bursting with beauty and use, will not return. In effect, it has been strip-mined, its gorgeous complexity boiled down into fuel for agribusiness (Gennino, 1990; Vidal, 2005).

This is not just a metaphor for, but a parallel process to, the contemporary cult of expertise which is munching its way through our culture. For every human activity, the goal of the expertise model is to operationalise it: boil it down to its 'essential components', extract correct ways of performing them, bullet point these methods, teach them, test them, assess them, monitor them. From a therapeutic point of view, this task of surveillance and control, this bringing of everything into the (strip)light of day, amounts to an impossible, hubristic project of abolishing the unconscious.

To apply to the field of therapy a model which opposes itself to what is unconscious, implicit and individual is a *reductio ad absurdum*. So for therapists not only to accept this but to welcome it, even ask for it, is not just a matter of turkeys voting for Christmas – it is more like turkeys inventing Christmas and writing the menu. Yet this is just what has happened. The UK government for years

---

2006. An article in the *European Journal of Psychotherapy and Counselling*, based on a talk given at Roehampton University as part of a conference on Therapeutic Training after Freud, where representatives of six umbrella organisations in the field of psychotherapy and counselling spoke.

showed no signs of interest in regulating psychotherapy; until very recently, at least, it insisted that it would only do so if a large majority of therapists and counsellors themselves requested it. It is still completely unclear what the majority of practitioners do want around regulation; but the largest organisations in the field have for some while been jumping up and down like schoolchildren shouting 'Us, sir! Please sir! Regulate us, sir!' They have also been conducting their own expertise-fest, trying to 'unify' and 'regularise' a field which is blatantly diverse and endlessly idiosyncratic. The expertise model objects to idiosyncrasy.

In becoming a system of expertise, therapy risks turning its back on a crucial aspect of its practice: what I have elsewhere called, following the language of anthropology and sociology, 'local knowledge' (Chapters 1, 6, 12 and 16 of this volume, drawing on Geertz, 1983; van der Ploeg, 1993; Wynne, 1995). While expertise is organised on a scientific or pseudo-scientific model, in terms which are standardised, quantifiable and (in theory) not open to subjective interpretation, local knowledges are essentially practical and qualitative, involving continuous negotiation between practitioner and environment. A classic example is farming or gardening, where detailed experience over time of local micro-conditions of weather and soil are at least as important as any general principles of agriculture. This is the way in which psychotherapy and counselling work. As many people have argued, therapy is at root far more a matter of experience, intuition and human sensitivity – wisdom, in fact – than one of technique and expertise (see, e.g., Lomas, 1999; Spinelli, 2002 – and many others).

The expertise model tends inexorably towards the position that there is a single activity of therapy, with variations which are not really worth making a fuss about. However, the local knowledge approach suggests that there is an inherent pluralism to the activity of therapy: each practitioner, and indeed each client – or even each session, generates a micro-variety of therapeutic practice which is, hopefully, the form best suited to that particular moment. It certainly seems to be the case that many different therapy approaches are effective, and that the relationship established between practitioner and client is the most crucial factor (Roth & Fonagy, 1996). But the fact that many kinds of therapy all work equivalently well does not mean they are all doing the same thing, or should be reduced to a single model.

Some of the value of therapy, in fact, is precisely in its *variousness* – because *people* are various, both clients and practitioners – each individual needs and benefits from a particular style of interaction, a unique quality of relationship. There is much evidence, both research-based and experiential, that many different trainings are effective in producing practitioners who can provide the conditions for good therapy. But each training is good *for specific therapists* – and clients. If we could try the impossible experiment of condiny all prospective psychoanalytic trainees to train in body psychotherapy, all the body psychotherapy trainees to train in CBT, and all the CBT trainees to train in psychoanalysis, then how many successfully trained practitioners would we expect to emerge?

However good trainings are, one will never be able to guarantee that they will produce only good therapists – or adequate therapists – or even *safe* therapists. In the final analysis it is the practitioners who need validating, not the trainings. On this issue the Independent Practitioners Network (IPN) is closer to BACP than to UKCP. However, we believe that hierarchical, top-down accreditation models, ultimately based on sophisticated forms of ticking the box, are not adequate for the purpose. Instead, we have developed a form of validation based on intensive, face-to-face peer interaction. (For more detail on this, see http://i-p-n.org.)

IPN has no individual members: its fundamental 'unit' is the *member group*, generally of between five and 10 practitioners. At any given moment IPN consists of a number of member groups connected to each other in a network of links, together with other groups aiming to reach this status, and individuals who may or may not be actively trying to form or join groups. Every full member group must have links with two other groups, and must publish an ethical statement for scrutiny by the whole network.

What creates an IPN group is the willingness of its members to *stand by each other's work*. Each member of a group has – by whatever means the group chooses – come to know and be known by each other member of the group, enough so that they trust their competence and motivation. This does not (of course) constitute a *guarantee* of their work – everyone makes mistakes – but competence and right motivation necessarily imply a willingness to face challenge. In the event of a conflict arising between a group member and a client, the other group members promise to commit themselves to sorting out whatever has gone wrong. For many people in IPN, standing by each other's work is the core of what we are about, and the process of achieving it is a deeply valuable experience.

There is no set procedure for reaching a position of 'standing by'. Every group does this in their own way. Some use fairly formal methods, whereby each person writes an account of their work, and the others 'rattle and shake' this account until they feel satisfied.

At the opposite pole, other groups simply develop an informal sense of each other as people and practitioners, through interaction, discussion of professional issues, and usually a lot of peer group supervision. (This is regarded as a valuable adjunct to, not a substitute for, individual supervision.)

Linking between groups happens in a parallel way. In order to agree a link, each group has to be willing to stand by the other group's *process*. They are not standing by the work of each member of that group; but they are agreeing that, if the other group hits difficulties, they will commit themselves to sorting out whatever has gone wrong. Again, this implies that the group has satisfied itself that its link group is operating satisfactorily – for example, it is meeting regularly, its members have engaged in appropriate processes in order to stand by each other's work, and this is ongoing, with a culture of challenge as well as of support. The sorts of situations in which a link group might become involved include a conflict between a member of the other group and one of their clients, or a conflict within the group itself. Clearly, a link group will normally depend upon the other group to inform it that its help is needed, but it is also possible for other interested parties to alert them.

One of the core functions of IPN is to facilitate the resolution of conflicts arising from its members' work, particularly conflicts with clients. These are very often framed as 'complaints', although IPN as a culture is unenthusiastic about this sort of language. Our goal in this situation is conflict resolution: not to render a legalistic verdict of 'guilty' or 'not guilty', but to reach, if possible, a sense of completion and moving on which is shared by all parties involved. This is obviously an ideal which cannot always be achieved; however, most dissatisfied clients are primarily simply looking for an apology, an acknowledgement of their hurt. If this can be brought about, then resolution is usually not far away.

For many people, the hardest thing to grasp about the Independent Practitioners Network is that it is a *network*: an organisation without a centre or periphery, a top or bottom. Although this closely resembles the universe, it is a way of organising which is not common in our society; it calls for a shift of attitude which can be painful. For example, although participants in IPN take on certain tasks, often there is no one whose job it is to meet our needs or respond to our requests. If we want something done, we frequently have to do it ourselves. Equally, in many situations there is no one to tell us what to do or not to do. We have to make our own choices, and take responsibility for what we decide. In many ways, IPN is as much a culture as an organisation: an attitude of mind rather than a set of rules.

The response of many practitioners on hearing about IPN – especially if they are active in other professional organisations – is something along the lines of: 'This is splendid, but obviously we couldn't apply it to the whole of psychotherapy and counselling.' What does this 'obviousness' imply about therapists and counsellors? We believe that IPN's model of validation, though certainly still imperfect, is more alive, more adequate for the task and, in fact, more rigorous than any other method so far proposed. Are the majority of practitioners supposed to be too lazy or too self-protective to use it? If so, is this a healthy state for the profession?

Even if the validation approach of IPN is not applied to the whole field – which we believe would be a splendid development – what is crucial for us is to retain the freedom to validate our own work in this way. Like many other therapists and counsellors, most of us in IPN do not see ourselves as 'mental health practitioners'; we object strenuously to being included in any medical model, whether it is the Health Professions Council or UKCP's proposed Mental Health Council. If any arrangements for psychotherapy and counselling need to be made at all (and this is by no means apparent), then they need to reflect the true variety of the field, which, as Denis Postle (1997/2011) has written, is much more like a rainforest than like a monoculture.

3

Looking Back

It was in 2023 that 'traditional' therapy and counselling finally became illegal under the new Social Fraud Act, leaving New Therapy in command of the field. Looking back, this had probably been inevitable since the state regulation of psychotherapy and counselling in 2014 (delayed from 2010 by the inevitable hitches and glitches): once the state took on the job of policing therapy, its definition of what was acceptable was bound to become increasingly draconian, as therapy was adjusted to fit concepts and standards which the civil service could comprehend and administer.

Perhaps 'procrustean' is a better word than 'draconian': gradually, all the bits of traditional therapy which could not readily be assessed or measured were lopped off, while simultaneously therapy was stretched to accommodate tasks which the state assigned to it. After the definition of successful therapeutic outcome was settled on as 'satisfaction of the client with their life, career and relationship status as it presently exists', the rest was inevitable: all of the required competencies of New Therapy tumbled into place, from psychopharmacy to neuropsychology. In practice, of course, the requirement for both New Therapist and client to fill in forms at the start and the end of each session, as well as after each moment of insight, meant that there was rarely time for the competencies to be exercised. However, this gave assurance that the competencies would not be exercised abusively; and the installation of CCTV cameras in every consulting room guaranteed that New Therapy was fully safe, while confidentiality was preserved by the fact that, because of financial constraints, no one was watching the CCTV footage, and only a software programme was analysing the audio for Danger Words like 'bomb', 'unconscious' or 'desire'.

The regulatory process was complemented by an ongoing redefinition of mental health, perhaps best illustrated by the appearance in 2022's *DSM-VI* of new psychopathologies like Climate Change Neurosis (characterised by a phobic reaction to our

---

2008. An editorial in *Psychotherapy and Politics International*, at a point when state regulation appeared imminent and almost inevitable.

wonderful new 100° summers and slug-killing -30° winters); Social Misalignment Syndrome (easily identified by unhappiness about anything); and Religious Mania (for example, being a practising Muslim). A generation of young New Therapists were trained, dedicated to helping their clients fit in, whatever the cost. As usual, the United States blazed the trail, following the publication of a huge body of new material on AVCT (Augmented View-Changing Technique, popularly known as Guantanamo Two).

What happened to the discredited traditional therapists? Some of them had been more or less underground since the later 2010s, changing their name to 'psychological helper', 'emotional supporter', or some other dubious term, before this option was removed by the Act of 2023. A very few served prison terms for illegal use of protected titles, or later for illegal practice of discredited techniques. But the great majority either silently retired or adapted to New Therapy – demonstrating, as the state saw it, the feebleness and fraudulence of their practice: if they were not even prepared to stand up for the value of their own work, then why should anyone else take them seriously?

In 2025, of course, the Revolution began ...

4

The Defeat of State Regulation in the UK

The recent abandonment by the UK government of plans for the state regulation of psychotherapy and counselling is very largely due to a grassroots opposition movement of practitioners. Nearly 3,000 signed an online petition against state regulation (a large number of practitioners and supporters also signed another, slightly more moderate, petition); money was raised for a challenge in the courts, where in a preliminary hearing the judge was deeply critical of the Health Professions Council (HPC), the body designated as regulator by the government; and before the full court hearing, the government announced that state regulation would not after all take place.

Certainly a number of other factors contributed to this splendid result; not least the election of a Conservative government with an ideological presumption against regulation (the initial plan for regulation was made under a Labour government). The HPC also made a number of stupid and arrogant tactical errors. However, bureaucratic inertia would almost certainly have meant that the plan went through, had it not been that the government was made aware of a profound and stubborn opposition among the practitioners themselves, many of whom committed themselves to withhold compliance from a regulatory scheme.

Perhaps the key event in the campaign against HPC regulation was the election by a landslide majority of Andrew Samuels, an opponent of HPC regulation, to the chair of the UK Council for Psychotherapy, one of the two major organisations in the field. The original intention was to use the election campaign as a platform for the argument against regulation; victory was a huge surprise, rocking the pro-regulation UKCP establishment to its foundations and demonstrating the massive grassroots antipathy to state control of our profession.

2012. Written for *The Script*, the journal of the International Transactional Analysis Association, who were keen to inform their readers struggling with regulation in other countries about what had happened in the UK. I felt justified in quoting at great length from the statement of the Alliance for Counselling and Psychotherapy, since it was largely drawn from a draft that I wrote.

The Defeat of State Regulation in the UK 23

The abandonment (at least for the time being) of state regulation needs to be seen in the context of the growing professionalisation of psychotherapy and counselling, which has inevitably led to the development of a new class of therapy oligarchs with a vested interest in installing mechanisms of command and control which they envisioned themselves operating. This class of oligarchs has suffered a double blow: first of all the state unexpectedly developed a plan for regulation which would have taken power away from the therapy organisations which they administered – and then they lost control of their own membership, who expressed a massive opposition to regulation itself.

This opposition was constellated by the spontaneous birth of a new organisation, the Alliance for Counselling and Psychotherapy, with the subtitle Against State Regulation. The Alliance's founding statement is worth repeating nearly in full:

> Many psychotherapists and counsellors are disturbed and unconvinced by current proposals for state regulation through the Health Professions Council (HPC). Nearly 1,300 [now nearly 3,000] have already signed a petition to that effect. Many feel that, for the sake of the profession and of their clients, they will be unable to comply with such regulation and will not join the proposed register. This is a message to the entire profession, inviting you to join with us in a cross-modality alliance to fight these plans. There are a number of reasons for opposition to HPC regulation, which are partly independent of each other: you need not agree with all of them in order to share our concerns about the implications of the proposed system. ...
>
> The argument for regulation by a state-sponsored body has never been made, but is simply assumed. There is no solid research demonstrating widespread abuse by practitioners; nor is there either research or argument to show that such regulation lessens abuse (doctors, for example, have been so regulated for many years, but shocking cases still occur regularly). Yet 'protection of clients' is still cited as the main grounds for state regulation. Despite the emphasis on 'evidence-based practice' which accompanies the demand for regulation, that demand is itself not evidence-based.
>
> Although many counsellors and psychotherapists work in medical settings, their work is not a branch of medicine nor an activity ancillary to medicine. Most forms of therapy do not focus exclusively on the relief of symptoms, but emphasise creating and exploring a relationship. If there is a goal, it is a general improvement in the quality of life (so that client

satisfaction, rather than the improvement of an isolated symptom, is the appropriate measure of effectiveness). Regulation through the HPC implies medical values and criteria which are in many ways antithetical to psychotherapy and counselling.

A majority of practitioners work full or part time in private practice. Their clients make decisions as responsible adults to come to them and to continue in therapy or to leave, and are able to seek advice or redress from a number of self-regulating professional bodies or from the legal system; they are in effect the practitioner's employer. State regulation is clearly inappropriate for an activity contracted voluntarily between adults. We support extending the private client's autonomy and freedom of choice to NHS and voluntary sector clients, rather than the reverse.

Many practitioners see their work as more an art than a science: a series of skilled improvisations in a relational context, where each client, and indeed each session, offers unique issues and demands unique responses. Such an activity cannot be captured by a list of 'competences', however elaborate; at best, such a list can offer only a parody of therapeutic practice. Yet regulation by civil servants, who themselves know nothing of the field they are regulating, demands an 'objective' version of our practice, even if this falsifies its nature. The inconvenient reality is that the field consists of many groups and individuals doing some of the same things in some of the same ways, but with many small and significant differences and with constant invention and variation – which has always driven advances in practice.

The therapeutic field is a rich and complex ecology, built up of many different approaches. This diversity is intrinsically valuable – since clients and their issues are equally varied – and is part of what we want to protect; however, from a regulatory point of view it is awkward and inconvenient, and needs to be ironed out. Good training helps the practitioner to develop their own unique style of work, rather than making them conform to a supposed 'best practice'. The proposed regulation bids fair to flatten this rich ecology into a monoculture, with devastating consequences for the profession and for its clients. Any attempt to impose a quasi-objective framework of standards and competences not only stifles creativity in the field, it also damages the therapeutic work with the client. In trying to apply a predetermined set of external principles to a particular individual, the practitioner must override the client's individuality and sacrifice the therapeutic process to the demands of a fixed technique. This is ethically unacceptable for the practitioner as well as therapeutically ineffective for the client.

The initiative to regulate psychotherapy and counselling is itself a symptom of our tick-box society: of an obsession with 'safety', a compulsion to monitor every activity, an illusory belief that everything can be brought under control. In many ways, psychotherapy and counselling inherently expose this illusion: they support us in tolerating uncertainty, difference, risk, and the unknown. Like many important activities, psychotherapy and counselling, though usually helpful, are inherently 'risky'; they cannot be made to conform to safety-first culture. HPC regulation will only strengthen the existing trend towards defensive practice – that is, practice which is more concerned to protect the practitioner from complaint than to help the client's growth and self-understanding.

The proposals for HPC regulation cannot be separated from the creation of National Occupational Standards for the field; the recent Skills for Health initiative to determine 'competences'; NICE clinical guidelines privileging a single form of 'evidence-based' therapy over all other modalities; and the so-called Improving Access to Psychological Therapies scheme. Between them, all of these developments promise to reduce access to long-term, relationally oriented therapy and counselling; to reduce client choice; to medicalise the field; and to rigidify training and inflate its cost, and hence the cost of therapy, making access even more difficult for the economically disadvantaged. HPC regulation is also likely to exclude from practice many part-timers and volunteers, as well as making it harder for counselling services using volunteers to survive.

HPC regulation could only be justified if the benefits could be shown to outweigh the drawbacks. For the reasons cited above, we believe that the damage caused to psychotherapy and counselling will be profound, and the benefits dubious and minor. There are clear alternatives available – some of them in concrete existence in the USA and Australia – which avoid the noxious elements of current proposals; but no effort has been made to examine them.

In this situation we are unable to stay silent. Our political, professional and personal conscience compels us to become guardians of the diversity and independence of psychotherapy and counselling, and to speak out on behalf of our own right to practise ethically and according to our best judgement; of the rich traditions of the discipline and of future generations of

> practitioners; and also of the clients who might seek to use our services now and in the future – their right of choice and their autonomy and responsibility. We will therefore do everything we can to oppose HPC regulation, and to alert others to the dangers involved. If these proposals become a reality, we do not expect to be able to consent, and are considering a position of principled non-compliance.
> (The Alliance for Counselling and Psychotherapy, http://www.allianceforcandp.org/)

This statement drew an immediate and powerful response, and was followed by two large and energetic public meetings. Several things about the Alliance are worth noting:

- It was an ad hoc grouping of practitioners from many different disciplines, most of whom had not previously known each other, which came together for one specific purpose.

- It had very open boundaries – anyone with energy for the task was welcome to move towards the centre and take an active role in decision making. Over the period of the campaign a number of people moved in and out of active involvement. While not exactly an equivalent of the Occupy movement, the Alliance was certainly a non-hierarchical and power-sharing movement.

- Although originally it was pretty much a single-issue group, activists were always aware that state regulation was closely linked to a number of other developments in the field all of which tend towards a more rigid, controlled and quasi-scientific version of psychotherapy and counselling. Hence the Alliance has not dissolved itself after winning one battle, but continues to exist under the new subtitle 'Supporting diversity, responsibility, autonomy and innovation in the psychological therapies', and to campaign in particular around the distorted notion of 'evidence-based practice' which dominates the state's relationship with the profession.

We cannot know what the future will bring. Western society currently has such a strong trend towards management and surveillance of all activities that it is hard to see how psychotherapy and counselling – so threatening to our culture's strange blend of individualism and conformity – can indefinitely resist. Perhaps, though, therapy can take on a role as spearhead and spokesperson for the resistance to surveillance and control which is also a strong and growing trend in Western society.

Part 2
The Nature of Therapy

5

The Battle for Reality

We bring certain power relationships into the therapy room with us, and discover certain power relationships already there, created by the nature of the work. I have discussed elsewhere (Chapter 17, this volume) specific issues around power which arise in the therapy or counselling relationship, deriving from the general social context where some people have more power than others. I want to focus here on power relations as they are structured by the therapy relationship itself. My argument is that practitioners need to be continuously alert to both sorts of power issue; but also, that we need to let go of any notion of eliminating or defusing such issues, and instead try to open them up to the transformative effects of awareness.

One of the most fundamental features of individual therapy or counselling is that there are exactly two people in the room (not counting ghosts, introjects, etc.) These two people will either agree about what is going on at any given moment, or they will disagree. Does each person have one vote on reality? Or is it more complex than that?

My suggested answer is that both are true. Each person has one vote; but at the same time, each person has a wide range of tactics available for claiming that their vote is worth more than the other's, and for influencing and manipulating how the other person uses their vote. Most obviously and notoriously, the practitioner can claim more authority to pronounce on the situation, because of their expertise, training, status, experience, and so on. This claim can be made explicitly, as used to be the norm, but it doesn't have to be: there are many subtle ways in which the therapist can imply that they know better than the client. In the heightened atmosphere of the therapy room, the least shift of intonation, the smallest pause or silence, every choice of which statements or actions of the client to respond to and which ones to ignore, all very effectively convey our views – even when we do not intend it (Totton, 2006a: 89ff).

2009. This is a version of an article which appeared in *Therapy Today* as 'Power in the Therapy Room', with some material removed which duplicated other chapters of this book.

The client can of course also try to dominate the situation; but the therapist has serious advantages from the start (Sands, 2000). She is on her home turf, both literally (even if not working from home, she is familiar with the environment) and in the sense that she has done this before, as many clients have not – and even if they have been in therapy before, they don't know how *this* therapist does things. From the moment they first enter the room, most clients are trying to work out what is expected of them and, generally speaking, to provide it. They are off balance; and without even realising it, the practitioner can exploit this.

I once saw a video of an initial interview between an analytic therapist and a prospective client. The therapist began by offering complete silence. After a few uncomfortable moments, the already flustered client asked something like, 'Should I tell you what my problem is, then?' Smiling gently, the therapist responded, 'Is there something else that you feel should happen?'

Within their own paradigm, the therapist was responding quite reasonably and appropriately. For an 'untrained' client, though, the response was bizarre and unnerving, apparently calculated to make them feel like an idiot, and to drain all spontaneity from the situation. However the kindly and empathetic humanistic therapist can be seen as offering an equally distorted interaction. To put the client at their ease, help them feel comfortable and cared for, offer them understanding and unconditional positive regard – all encourages the client to feel grateful and indebted, and to avoid anything which might cause this comfort to be withdrawn.

The client's dependence on the counsellor or therapist is obvious. But the therapist is equally dependent on the client: not only (in private practice) for their money, but also and perhaps even more importantly for their positive feedback. Offering therapy is a very scary and insecure experience, even if we have been doing it so long that we aren't often conscious of the scariness; and we need our clients to appreciate what we are doing, to value us, like us – even to admire us. Some practitioners instead deal with the anxiety of the therapist's role by despising and denigrating their unfortunate clients.

These needs and anxieties on both sides of the room offer fuel for all sorts of complex power plays, manipulations, blackmails, seductions and seizing of the moral high ground, as part of the attempt on both sides to gain the other person's acquiescence in a particular view of what is going on in the room and in the client's past and present life. Generally speaking, the therapist wants the client to agree that they have problems, that the therapist to some extent understands those problems (because they fit with the therapist's theoretical paradigm), and that the two of them are working together in a way that will tend to resolve the problems. What the client wants the therapist to agree about is generally more individual and complex – perhaps, for example, that the client has been badly treated by other people; perhaps that the meeting between client and therapist is a very special one, even a romantic one, perhaps that the client is a truly exceptional person. The possibilities are endless; and of course the therapist may hold equivalent notions, often unconsciously. There is generally a real tussle going on.

I am not attacking anyone by pointing out the shape of the therapy situation, far less am I criticising the nature of psychotherapy and counselling; I am simply pointing out some of the feelings that inevitably arise when two human beings come together in this context. My interest is in what we can usefully do in relation to this. I suggest that the inevitable power struggles over the reality of the situation should not be ignored, smoothed over, or subjected to attempts to fix them. Instead, they should be identified, acknowledged and explored, as crucial resources in understanding and unfolding the client's process.

A big part of the wound which most of us bring to therapy or counselling is the sense that our experience has been ignored and overridden. We can respond to this wound in all sorts of different ways, and find many different ways to hold on to our own sense of reality; but a core experience for most people – not surprisingly, considering dominant ideas about children and childcare – is of having our reality denied.

This might seem to suggest that the therapist's job is to comfort and soothe the wound, and to offer a reparative experience of being heard and accepted. And this is indeed a very important part of many therapeutic relationships. However, it is not enough. A loving and empathic therapy will not on its own enable the client to access the pattern of their distress; in a sense it may even help them to cover it over. There is little that we can do *deliberately* to change this – by being a nasty and dominating therapist, for example! All we can do is to make room for the pattern of distress to express itself; which it will necessarily do *through the therapist*.

I am talking here about *enactment* (Aron, 2001: Ch 7): the now widely recognised fact that therapists and counsellors can find themselves irresistibly dreamt up to take the role of the oppressor and wounder from their client's story, and to repeat – hopefully in a relatively gentle and symbolic form – the traumatic experience which the client has been struggling to process. The more we try to avoid this, the more it is forced upon us. And the means of enactment are readily available to us, in the difficult power relations of the therapeutic situation, and in the wider social context of power-inflected rank differences which surround and invade the therapy room.

So what is to be done? With enactments in general, and perhaps especially with enactments of wounds around rank and power (remember that children suffer greatly from low rank), the first issue is to recognise and acknowledge what has happened; the next issue is to distinguish between shame and apology. We need to apologise for what we have done, while recognising that it has been thrust upon us by the drive to heal old wounds. We must also recognise that enactments use the therapist's weak spots: if I have any traces of arrogance, boredom or contempt, of racism, sexism or classism – and who doesn't? – these will be activated on behalf of the client's process.

More generally, I am suggesting that the struggle in the therapy room over the definition of reality is not pathological, but healthy; and that it deserves recognition and support. Rather than trying secretly or unconsciously to manipulate each other, the client and therapist can negotiate, argue, wrestle together over how to understand their experience of each other. This may be a challenging process; but who will find it more threatening, the client or the practitioner?

6

Two Ways of Being Helpful

It's called speciation: the process whereby two isolated populations of the same creature gradually diverge and, through natural selection and/or genetic drift, become two different kinds. Is something like this happening to therapy? Are subpopulations of therapists who inhabit different environments adapting to those environments, and developing two quite distinct activities, both valid and valuable in their own context, and both unfortunately going by the same name of 'therapy'? My suggestion is that by identifying these two different groups, and understanding what makes them different and why those differences exist, we might be able to avoid a lot of the bickering and name-calling which plagues the field, and ultimately to agree on peaceful coexistence, each in our own ecological niche.

I'm not sure how helpful the biological analogies are. I am trying to find a way to talk about the difference between two ways of doing therapy, which I have described (for example in my BACP keynote address, on which this article draws: Chapter 16, this volume) as the 'expert systems' approach and the 'local knowledge' approach. Expert systems therapy is the more recent arrival on the scene. It has evolved to cope with an environment that demands expertise, demonstrated partly through qualifications and partly through quantified research into outcomes and effectiveness.

This is an environment, also, in which both clients and purchasers are demanding – are encouraged to demand – maximum amelioration of distress in minimum time. In other words, the appropriate users are people who don't prioritise self-knowledge and psychological exploration. As Arnold Mindell puts it, they aren't members of the Growers' Club: 'Like most club members everywhere, members of the growers' club are prejudiced against non-members' (Mindell, 1988: 41). They are individuals with other, equally valid focuses to their lives, who simply want to be able to

---

2004. Another article from *Therapy Today* (*CPJ* as it was then), raising a theme which still seems important to me now: that two very different activities are taking place under the title of 'therapy and counselling', and that to recognise and allow for this might be good for everyone involved.

get on with things. Expert systems therapy, therefore, is a lean, mean evolutionary machine, which avoids detours and distractions, and privileges symptom removal over the uncovering of meaning. Its practitioners are often enormously skilful at what they do, by virtue of their tight and creative focus on effective technique.

Local knowledge therapy has evolved in a very different world, one in which clients – usually self-financing – have chosen to seek, alongside and even sometimes in preference to symptom removal, *understanding* of their symptoms, placing them within the wider context of their life as a whole, their family and social networks, the entire social and cultural framework, and indeed human existence in general. Local knowledge therapy is in this sense anything but local! The name, borrowed from sociology and anthropology, refers to a reliance on intuition and wisdom in preference to technique and research: an emphasis on *self*-knowledge for both practitioner and client.

Clearly local knowledge therapy is enormously privileged in what it is able to do, in terms of available resources and the pace at which it is therefore possible to work. Expert systems therapy operates at a point of convergence between, on the one hand, clients who often want to avoid dependence on their therapist and return as fast as possible to a state of ordinary functioning; and on the other hand, service providers who need quick and cost-effective ways of restoring their users as fast as possible to a state of ordinary functioning. No one in this context is in a position to question what exactly 'ordinary functioning' implies.

Local knowledge therapy, however, by virtue of its privileged situation, is able to ask these sorts of questions; is able, for example, to use the values and understandings of therapy as a measure against which ideas of 'ordinary functioning', and other social norms and standards, can be critiqued. Many therapists feel that the sorts of unhappiness which they see in their clients are in large part the *creation* of the dominant social order (very often mediated through the family): that it is the way in which we all live – together, of course, with the difficulties which are inherent in embodied existence – that makes us 'ill'. If this is our understanding of things, then we are necessarily humble about our own function.

That function is nonetheless real and important; but very different, I suggest, from the function of expert systems therapy, which is explicitly to *help* people deal with the effects of the way in which we live – or of their brain chemistries, or poor strategic choices, depending on which paradigm one uses. It employs a considerable array of techniques to help clients manage their distress, ideally to such an extent that they no longer experience it and are able to operate successfully according to their own conscious preferences.

This is clearly an important, respectable and comprehensible goal. The goal of local knowledge therapy is much harder to articulate, which is perhaps one reason why the situation has become so confused. I suggest that this way of working is not actually about helping; or rather, paradoxically, it knows that in order to be *helpful* it has to avoid as far as possible actually *helping*. I suggest that local knowledge therapy, in all its many forms and subforms, is above all *a practice of truth*, which aims to study and understand whatever is actually going on, in the client and in their past and present life, and in the consulting room. Within this paradigm, for the therapist to attempt direct helping is to abandon the project of understanding – at least temporarily, and often with long-term damage to that project. A helper identifies with a particular point of view; and, as I shall go on to discuss, this identification works against understanding.

(The paradox actually cuts even deeper: we do of course offer help, at times of real crisis or even at other moments if there is a deep impulse to do so. Sometimes help is necessary to make it possible for the therapy to continue. But even apart from this, there are times when if we didn't try to help we would not be human; and it is only through our humanity that we can practise therapy. In order to be therapeutic in the sense I am exploring, however, that impulse to help, and the effects of our helping, need to become part of what we are studying.)

Local knowledge therapy, then, is intrinsically concerned with truth and its consequences, untruth and its consequences, and how to distinguish the two. It is by no means the only such practice; but unlike science or philosophy, the truth it studies is not just rational but *emotional*. And unlike religion, for example, local knowledge therapy also tells us, truthfully, that no truth is absolute – that truth is not singular but plural and contingent, and therefore subject to negotiation. All knowledge, that is, is wholly 'local' rather than universal.

This is perhaps the greatest realisation of modernity, a profoundly difficult, profoundly transformative piece of news: there is no absolute truth, but instead a potentially infinite number of relative truths, truth from particular perspectives. Realising this, we are liberated from the illusory responsibility to determine what is absolutely true; freed to take our own side, support our own truth, as part of the deep democracy of negotiated reality.

Our work in the consulting room offers a direct window onto this. We work in a dyad where each of two people has a say on what constitutes 'reality'; so that agreement can very often only be reached by negotiation. Both parties naturally try to control this negotiation with every technique at their command so as to influence the other person's view; and exploring the techniques which the client uses, and the ways in which they expect and fear that the therapist will try to control their view of reality, is a core element in the therapeutic work. In this way, very early hurts around power, autonomy and validation can be re-experienced and transformed; but if mishandled, they can also be reinforced.

The most obvious way, it seems to me, that as therapists we can mishandle the situation, is to claim that because we *are* therapists we have a greater say on the reality of the situation. This is a mistake to which the expert systems approach is perhaps rather vulnerable: the claim that my expertise, my specialist knowledge, my insight into the human heart and its foibles, entitles me to an extra vote. Unfortunately, irritatingly, this is no more true of the therapy relationship than it is of a parliamentary election.

Inventing a new creole

I want to offer an account of what happens in a successful local knowledge therapeutic interaction, using the analogy of what happens when two language groups encounter each other. If the members of one language group are considerably more powerful than the other group – for example, if they have guns and the others don't – then the second group simply learns the first group's language. But if the two groups are roughly equal in power, or if each wants something the other group can provide, then a new form of communication develops between them: what is known as a *pidgin*, an artificial language using an extremely simple syntax, and vocabulary drawn from the languages of both groups.

A pidgin is not a natural language. To put it simply, you could say that it isn't alive: it won't develop, generate new words and concepts, become a medium for poetry. However, once children are born who grow up speaking it, a pidgin is transformed: it becomes what is called a *creole*, a new natural language as creative and infinite in its potential as any other language on earth. This, I suggest, is what needs to happen in therapy. First of all the client and practitioner create a pidgin, put together from elements of the language which each person brings with them. But if there is a fertile exchange between therapist and client, a creative intercourse, then a new language is born, a creole, a vessel for new thoughts and feelings that did not pre-exist in either original tongue.

What much more often happens, I'm afraid, is that the therapist overawes the client – who may well want to be overawed! – into *learning the therapist's language*. And, of course, speaking the therapist's language, the client will only tell us what we know already. This lays therapy open to the profound and valid criticism made by Fliess to Freud before psychotherapy even officially existed: 'The reader of thoughts merely reads his own thoughts into other people' (Masson, 1985: 447). The truth is that, being human, we cannot know what our clients are thinking. All we can do, if we insist that thought and knowledge must come together, is to persuade them to think what we know.

Making the client speak our language is only one of many possible ways in which, as therapists, we can re-enact our clients' early trauma. Most children grow up forced to speak their parents' language, not only literally but also symbolically. Most children, I think, have painful experiences of being misunderstood, or worse, not listened to in the first place. In this area in particular, but also in a number of other ways, it is almost certain that at some point we will repeat our clients' early painful experiences. This can be minimised, but not avoided. And it is the way in which we negotiate this painful and difficult situation – our ability, if you come right down to it, to identify and acknowledge our mistake and to apologise – which decides whether the therapeutic encounter will be a reinforcement of early experiences of powerlessness, or a site where new experiences of empowerment can take place.

This is a very different conception of psychotherapy from that of expert systems approaches. And it is that very difference, I think, which can allow us all to coexist – through the realisation that although we all (currently) call ourselves therapists, what we are doing is in fact quite different. We can, if we choose, both accuse each other of 'not really doing psychotherapy'. Or we can recognise that, by accident of history – more specifically, by the opening up of a fault line that has always existed within the practice of therapy – two different activities have ended up bearing the same name. Maybe one or both of us will have to give up the name. But these two activities – the practice of psychological truth, and the practice of psychological helping – are both worthy, both valuable, and should both continue.

7

Depending on Each Other

It is a fundamental fallacy to believe that it is possible by the elaboration of machinery to escape the necessity of trusting one's fellow human beings.
(Clement Attlee)

The fear of dependency

Over the past few years I've become aware of a new attitude among prospective clients – confirmed by several colleagues and supervisees. Although their problems are in much the same range that I am used to encountering, people who contact me show an increased reluctance to commit themselves to ongoing weekly psychotherapy – a reluctance which is often based on *a fear of becoming dependent*. Their hope, it seems, is to have as little therapy as possible, for as short a time as possible, so that they can escape before dependency becomes an issue. Being dependent on a therapist is assumed to be a bad thing, a self-evidently good reason for avoiding long-term therapy. Very often, they speak of what friends and family have said to them about the dangers of depending on a therapist.

In this chapter, I want to think about the various factors behind this attitude; and also, to counter it with a robust defence of dependency. Depending on others is utterly inevitable, a central aspect of the human condition: it comes with the package of embodiment. But this is not bad news! Depending on other people can be, I believe, one of the best experiences that make up life – just as celebrating our independence can equally be a peak experience. If this is true, then we need to consider what shifts in our culture are producing the anti-dependent attitude I have described.

This anti-dependent attitude is not confined to prospective clients: it has been taken up by a number of practitioners. Some of

---
2006. Also from *Therapy Today*, and using the Attlee quote which has already appeared in Chapter 2 with a rather different emphasis.

these (e.g. Bates & House, 2003) are coming from a radical position which critiques the power imbalance of the therapeutic relationship – a critique with which I largely agree; I believe, though, that by foregrounding and examining power issues in therapy, we can make them into a useful and empowering feature of the therapeutic encounter (Totton, 2006a; Chapter 5, this volume). The other main group of practitioners who take an anti-dependency stance are proponents of brief and solution-focused therapies; and here the arguments about power are knotted up with practical issues, financial constraints and pressures which militate against long-term intensive therapy. If you are only offering six or 12 sessions, dependency is indeed an undesirable development. Some at least of the arguments around dependency seem to me to be *ex post facto* justifications of the unavoidable.

Both sets of arguments, though, need placing in the wider context of the ever-increasing value which our society puts on independence, autonomy, self-sufficiency. Once one becomes sensitised to it, the anti-dependency assumption is visible everywhere, in all registers of discourse and fields of life. In a quick trawl through the Guardian website (www.guardian.co.uk) I found the following, ranging from international politics, through the climate crisis, to social policy and disability:

> *welfare dependency that breeds poverty and inter-ethnic strife ... the financial dependency on America that hobbled Macmillan and Wilson ... the growing foreign dependency of European energy supply ... without growth, the country will not emerge out of its culture of dependency ... the purpose of state funding is to avoid dependency on a small number of individuals ... reduce your dependency on mains water ... people will be thus empowered to make the move away from dependency on council-run services ... a culture of dependency by the Iraqi police and security forces ... cycles of dependency ... ending a dependency culture ... many charities are guilty of 'mollycoddling' homeless people and creating a dependency culture ... the new era of means-testing and tax credits has created a new form of dependency ... physical impairment need not and should not equal dependency ... lessening dependency on fossil fuels ...*

I want to underline the assumption built into these quotations that dependency is a bad thing. Many of the arguments could equally well be made the other way around: not 'reduce your dependency on mains water' but 'let yourself depend on rainwater'. It reaches an extreme with the suggestion that 'physical impairment need not equal dependency': plainly a fantasy, the actual point being that dependency on others need not be demeaning or restrictive.

Anti-dependency is not just a matter of rhetoric: it affects the concrete parameters of our lives. We live in smaller and smaller units, tending towards aloneness – the government has announced a housing crisis because for the next 20 years the number of households in Britain is expected to rise by around 200,000 a year, of which 150,000 will be due to a higher number of single people living alone (Seager, 2006). Environmentally motivated attempts to create multiple-occupancy car lanes come up against the stubborn unwillingness of people to share their cars, their personal space: in the US in 2000, only 9 per cent of work trips were made in multi-occupant vehicles, compared with 16 per cent in the 1980s (Poole & Orski, 2000: 20).

As Avrum Weiss says:

> When we become ill, we try to manage our affairs so that we will not become 'a burden to anyone,' depriving not only ourselves of the love and comfort that may be necessary for recovery but also depriving our loved ones of the opportunity to give in a meaningful way and to feel helpful. When we are in financial trouble, we borrow money from a bank because it's 'a bad idea to borrow from friends.' When we are sad, or in pain, we isolate ourselves, convinced that no one would want to be around someone who feels the way we do. We create social institutions (Medicare, insurance, social service agencies, psychotherapy, etc.) to protect ourselves from the experience of dependency.
>
> (Weiss, 2002: 8)

Notice that Weiss includes therapy among the institutions which shield us from dependency. Certainly therapy can be positioned as a substitute for personal intimacy, a sort of prosthetic family connection – far safer than real intimacy, because no demands will be made on the client. This allows the apparatchiks of national and international psychotherapy organisations to move in with claims of unique expertise: psychotherapy is a 'new paradigm for living' and will provide 'the replacement of old religious and spiritual values'. 'Ordinary people's lives are too cluttered to pay such attention to self and others', so therapists must take on the task; 'as women are now absorbed into the workforce the function of holding individuals' wellbeing safe needs to be taken care of by professional structures' (all quotations from Tantam & van Deurzen, 1998: 131–2).

The privileging of independence is not (yet) universal, but specific to white mainstream culture. Ethnic minority cultures generally are more interdependent than European American cultures (Sue, Ivey & Pedersen, 1996). African American, American Indian, Asian American, and Latino American cultures all privilege interpersonal relationships and group identity, rather than the autonomy of the individual (Hall, 2001). In Japan, the infant is considered to be completely independent at birth, and the cultivation of the capacity for appropriate dependency is one of the important tasks of the parents (Kobayashi, 1989). The Japanese psychoanalyst Takeo Doi (2002) has identified as a key feature of Japanese culture the quality of 'amae', meaning a strong need to be approved of and cared for by authority figures; this is one basis for the tendency in East Asian societies to emphasise affective ties, role fulfilment, and self-cultivation.

Even within white mainstream culture, the stress on independence is a gendered one. A number of feminist writers, notably those associated with the Stone Institute in the USA, argue that women grow through and toward relationship, rather than toward self-sufficiency and separation. This makes women particularly vulnerable to the pain of disconnection and loss; and it is argued that therapy for women therefore needs to be relational in its emphasis, offering transformative connection to help clients move out of the suffering caused by disconnection and isolation (Eichenbaum & Orbach, 1983; Jordan, 1995; Jordan et al, 1991; Solomon, 1994). I believe that this does not apply only to women, although it may be more masked in men.

Anti-dependency has a powerful shadow side – seen, for example, in the strong tendency to view those who are understood to be more *dependent*, for example women and children, as also *inferior*. A different sort of shadow is the tendency to export dependent aspects of our existence elsewhere, or make them invisible: as Isobel Conlon points out (personal communication), the whole stance of 'independent' consumerism is based on massive personal debt, dependence on banks and other financial institutions (the average UK household owes £47,546, with every adult owing an average of £25,195: Osborne, 2006). Much the same is true of 'independent' nation states dependent on the global economy, and 'independent' drivers and fliers dependent on petroleum technologies. And, of course, it is people's unwillingness to pay taxes towards the common good that creates the financial constraints out of which short-term therapy and counselling have developed.

None of us are independent; as John Donne said long ago, no one is an island, but 'a piece of the Continent, a part of the main'.

The fact of embodied existence makes us dependent on everything we need in order to stay embodied: not only the physical needs of the organism for food, water, air, shelter and so on, but also its equally urgent *emotional* needs, for touch, holding, psychological contact, communication, understanding. Like doing without physical nourishment, doing without emotional nourishment will be damaging; and part of the damage is our adaptation to scarcity, taking on the illusion of independence as a defence against vulnerability.

Avrum Weiss describes this outcome as 'excessive psychological self-reliance or the impaired capacity for dependency' (Weiss, 2002: 7). I am suggesting that this state is becoming endemic, and culturally dominant: an inability to lean on others, created by fear of emotional abandonment and deprivation, is being turned into a pseudo-virtue of illusory independence. If this is right, surely therapists and counsellors have a responsibility to speak out against such a process. We are in a position to know that *depending on someone who is dependable* is a healing experience, allowing enormous relief of tension, relaxation from the often unconscious sense that one is all alone and that nothing and no one can be relied on. In my own discipline of body psychotherapy, we distinguish two sorts of groundedness: *vertical grounding*, the ability to stand on my own two feet, and *horizontal grounding*, the ability to lie back and let myself be held up by the earth. Both are important, and in fact interdependent: each supports the other.

Interdependence

Interdependence, mutual support, is really at the centre of what I am talking about. Dependence seldom actually runs in one direction only. Even in the classic dyad of mother and baby, while the baby is plainly dependent on the mother for physical and emotional survival, the mother is generally deeply dependent on the baby as well – this is what we mean by 'bonding'. Mutuality of need and trust is also what makes grown-up relationships work – as is well argued in extensions of Bowlby's and Ainsworth's attachment theory to adults by writers like Hazan and Shaver (1987). And at several removes interdependence, mutual need and trust, is also the foundation of the social bond, the glue which holds society together.

In his book *The Presenting Past: The Core of Psychodynamic Counselling and Therapy* (Jacobs, 2005), Michael Jacobs synthesises attachment theory and other psychodynamic approaches into a model organised around three developmental positions which he calls *dependency, autonomy* and *interdependence*. To help us think about these issues I want to privilege interdependence, and to add another position, *manipulation*, or distrustful dependency; so that we can create a relationship triangle like this:

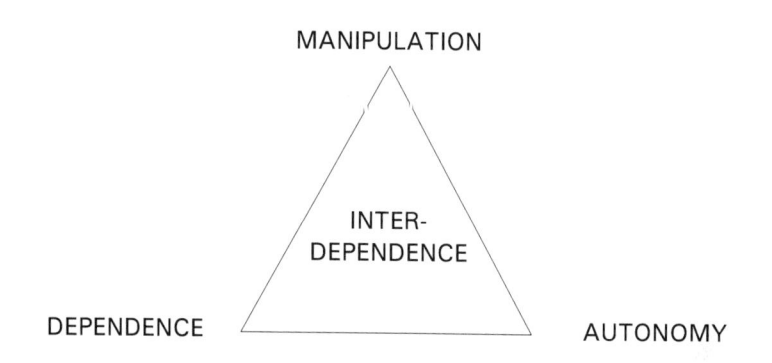

```
                    MANIPULATION
                         /\
                        /  \
                       /    \
                      / INTER-\
                     /DEPENDENCE\
                    /            \
DEPENDENCE         /_____\         AUTONOMY
```

Each person's preferred relationship style could be placed somewhere within this triangle, indicating a particular balance between dependency, autonomy and manipulation – a particular way of missing or approaching interdependence, the ability to both lean on the other and be leant on by them. (This diagram relates closely to the Contact Triangle discussed in Chapter 21, this volume.) In my view, interdependence is not only a crucial skill for personal relationships; it is also an essential way of understanding and relating to both the social sphere and the ecosphere. The illusion of independence damages the individual and those who come into contact with them. It also damages society as a whole, and the whole planetary biosphere, if people believe that they can take without giving, and that taking does not make them dependent on the sources from which they take.

As usual, therefore, I am arguing that therapy contains an inherent political dimension. Offering our clients the opportunity to depend on someone who is dependable is offering them entrance into a different perception of the world, which in turn suggests a different way of relating to society and to the planet. As I have suggested, it also helps create a firm foundation for genuine independence – which is always, in reality, *inter*dependence. In a society trending towards anti-dependence, therapists and counsellors need to speak up for the importance of depending on each other.

8

'Intimacy Took Place'

Intimacy is in many ways right at the heart of what we do as therapists. But it is also right at the dangerous edge, in the specific sense in which Arnold Mindell (1985: 25–7) uses the term: an *edge* is the limit of a person's comfort zone, the aspect of our experience which challenges us to change and grow. While achieved intimacy is often profoundly comfortable, I suspect that to be confronted with the possibility of intimacy in any context tends to take us to an edge. I will say why I think this is so in a moment. And Mindell suggests that when we approach an edge, we encounter threatening and critical figures, either internally or projected onto the external world.

In therapy we are constantly in situations where intimacy is at least a possibility; even once achieved it often feels fragile or intermittent. I suggest that the edge figures Mindell speaks of are very much present in our work, in three main forms: the Dangerous Therapist, the Dangerous Client, and what I call the Therapy Police.

The Dangerous Therapist is the most well known of these. Most discussions of regulation, complaints procedures and so on either start out from or very soon arrive at issues of intimacy and its abuse. Almost always this focuses on sexual abuse. 'Intimacy Took Place' was the expression used when I was young in newspapers and law courts to signify 'they had sex'. This identification of intimacy and sex creates problems for therapy, where intimacy frequently 'takes place' but sex, hopefully, never does. It also contradicts ordinary experience, which shows us that sex often happens without intimacy and intimacy often happens without sex. Although the phrase is no longer current, it seems to me that the counterfactual identification of intimacy with sex is still very much present in our culture. We shall be encountering this identification in one form or another all day. It is behind the identification of the therapist who offers intimacy with the dangerous therapist who offers, or even demands, sex.

2010. A lightly edited transcript from a workshop for BACPA Gloucestershire, which I have also given in a couple of other places.

Also very much present, though, is the edge figure of the Dangerous Client, the client who demands kinds of intimacy, up to and including sex, which are threatening to the therapist. The Dangerous Client has an interesting resemblance to the Dangerous Baby featured in a certain kind of childcare discourse, the baby who tries to have her parent 'wrapped round her little finger', who manipulates and seduces and seeks attention. With both baby and client, we might well ask, 'what is so wrong with seeking attention?' The figure of the dangerous client draws forth a response of what is known as 'defensive practice' – styles of working which are shaped not by the client's needs, but by the therapist's need not to have a complaint made about them. Another sort of dangerous therapist, it seems, is the therapist who is weak, vulnerable to seduction and manipulation. We need to be tough, to offer tough love.

Defensive practice defends not only against the client, but also against the imagined criticism of one's peers, one's profession, and society – all of which can be summed up in the image of the Therapy Police. The Therapy Police monitor our practice through invisible CCTV cameras. When the Dangerous Therapist seems to manifest, they smash down the door and storm into the room, dragging us off to suffer in Azkaban. So our ultimate dread is the imagined Dangerous Client who manipulates us into 'inappropriate' intimacy, and then shops us to the Therapy Police.

What, then, is 'appropriate' intimacy? And should we try to define the term itself? Looking at the dictionary, as people usually do when preparing this sort of talk, it's clear that intimacy relates to being on the *inside* of something: a body, a group, a family, a relationship, an understanding. We offer our clients, I think, the possibility of being inside something with us; or at any rate, we offer them our willingness to try to be inside something with them.

The idea of being inside something together makes me think of a supervisee who found herself under the table with her client, in a little tent created by the tablecloth. I say 'found herself' because she was a little surprised, and anxious; but I don't want to give the impression that this was an impetuous move, it was thought through and talked through, and very helpful for a therapeutic relationship that had become rather stuck. It's a good example of the *child-to-child transference* which has been hardly talked about as a part of therapy – the two kids whispering together under the table and peering out at the adult world. I think what surprised my supervisee was that she had had the nerve to agree to something which in some ways feels as shocking and transgressive, as much in need of policing, as intimate touch.

Let's pause for a moment, and each of you find a neighbour and talk about your reaction to this image of client and therapist under the table.

I want to ask you to think about how intimate or otherwise that conversation felt?

So, we've looked briefly at two sorts of intimacy that can arise in therapy, at least in fantasy: sexual intimacy, and child-to-child intimacy (which can of course also be sexual, but child sexuality is radically different from adult sexuality). There is a third sort which gets a great deal more theoretical air-time than either of these, and that is *parent–child intimacy*. There is a very prevalent notion among therapists, sometimes explicit and sometimes not, that an experience of parent–child intimacy is the gold standard, something to be welcomed, indeed aimed for, and that it has an inherently healing and reparative function.

I feel very suspicious of all this. Certainly it's occasionally true; but we mustn't lose sight of the reality that in the therapy context parent–child intimacy, just like erotic or child-to-child intimacy, is a fiction, a fantasy; and one, I suggest, which is far more comfortable and convenient for the therapist than other fictional models of intimacy which can arise. In the role of parent, the therapist can rest safely in their identification as bigger, wiser, stronger – as the source rather than the recipient of reward and punishment. No wonder that it is our favoured model!

Ultimately all of these models of therapeutic intimacy are transferential fictions. In fact we can think of transference in therapy precisely as a response to the offer and experience of intimacy. In order to manage the intensity of the experience, we as clients try to fit it into a previously known category – 'This is just like having a parent, just like having a lover, just like having a childhood friend'. Transference is thus a reaching out towards the other, making a bridge – and at the same time a *misrecognition*, a resistance to the uniqueness of what is happening by treating it as a repetition of something else. And that 'something else' may well be a negative experience rather than a positive one, or combine negative and positive elements – all of which will then be 'found' in the relationship with our therapist.

As we all know, transference is enormously helpful, because it allows early wounds to reappear in a concrete form in the therapeutic relationship – specifically, wounds around intimacy. And it's lucky that transference is helpful, because despite the early hopes of psychoanalysis, we have no way of getting rid of it! – And no way either to get rid of the countertransference responses of the therapist. But it is, I think, right for the therapist to hold in her awareness, at the same time as experiencing these misrecognitions in her client and in herself, that they are misrecognitions: to hold in awareness that what she is really offering the client is not a parent, not a lover, not a child companion, but something quite distinct which we can call *therapeutic intimacy*.

I'm going to break again here, and ask you to go into groups of three and to each share experiences which come to mind of these four various flavours of intimacy in a therapeutic context: sexually charged, parent–child, child-to-child, and therapeutic. These can be either from your experience as a practitioner, or as a client. We could obviously spend a great deal of time on this, but I'm going to ask you to do what you can in about five minutes for each person – just to scan quickly through your memories and see what comes up.

Before this exercise I suggested that therapeutic intimacy is something quite distinct from the various more familiar versions of intimacy with which we confuse it. In fact it is something new on the face of the planet: an authentic openness which is also time limited, asymmetrical, and, frequently, paid for. All of these features can create frustration, rage and confusion: how many clients compare us with prostitutes? But the time limit and the payment, beyond the fact that they make it possible for us to do the job, also benefit the client: unlike other situations of intimacy, this one entails no further responsibility towards us than keeping appointments, paying us, and leaving in time. In a very curious way, therapy actually embodies many men's fantasy of what prostitution *should* be – without the exploitation, the danger and the brutality. Also, of course, without the sex, which is what many men seek from prostitution; but it is also well known that for many clients of prostitutes it is important to be able to imagine that the woman, or man, wants to be with them, cares about them, sympathises with them, understands them.

I'm not aware that anyone has really thought deeply about the uniqueness of therapeutic intimacy – about what it is that we and our clients are inside together. From a certain point of view, psychotherapy works by temporarily substituting its own 'impossible demands' for those which we experience in life in general (cf. Chapter 12, this volume). The template for this is what Freud called 'free association', taken in a very broad sense as the support and encouragement of spontaneity. One function of the request to free associate is to highlight its impossibility: to make us aware of our resistances and inhibitions – and, more deeply, of our lack of title, so to speak, in what is said, thought and felt: that the 'I' who is supposed to be the source and origin of our thoughts and words is in reality a fiction, an artefact. Very few therapists these days work explicitly with free association, which is perhaps a shame; but many of us certainly put a steady, implicit pressure on clients to respond spontaneously and authentically, which has the same effect.

Again, let's try a simple experiment. Turn to your neighbour, and take three minutes each to try to share everything which comes into your mind. If 'nothing comes to mind', then you are either dead; or enlightened; or censoring yourself. Censoring yourself is perfectly natural, and I'm not trying to stop you doing it; just to help you be aware of how much of it you do.

The impossibility of saying or doing 'whatever comes into your head' reveals the impossibility of accounting for oneself, the impossibility of manifesting both consistency and spontaneity. We cannot deliberately be spontaneous, because we can never be anything else but spontaneous. The more we try to be spontaneous, the more stiff and anxious we get! – which of course doesn't mean that we are no longer spontaneous, just that we don't feel spontaneous. Equally, we feel inconsistent, because we imagine consistency as being a state in which everything is available to consciousness and fits together seamlessly. We also confuse this with authenticity. But there is no such state. The consistent thing about us is that we are in a process of continual and uneven change, so that different parts of us are occupying different positions. We tend to struggle desperately against this reality as we try to meet the demand for spontaneous authenticity which we experience in therapy.

What makes all this both bearable and useful, I suggest, is the fact that it happens in a context of intimacy. What therapist and client are inside together is a continuous shared struggle to relate authentically, to uncover and acknowledge the ways in which each person is defending themselves against the other and seeking to gain control of the relationship. This is far more naked than taking our clothes off!

I want to move on now to saying something about embodiment and intimacy, and something about erotic charge in therapy. These two themes are obviously linked. You may notice that I have shifted from using the word 'sexual' to using the word 'erotic': this is not a euphemism, but a way of emphasising a distinction that I think is crucial to our work.

One clear fact about human animals is that we have bodies – in fact, we *are* bodies; something that therapy has not always been eager to acknowledge. Working therapeutically in full awareness that there are two bodies in the room can be extremely challenging:

those two bodies can have all sorts of powerful feelings about each other – can want to do all sorts of things to each other – and it would often be easier to keep a distance of dissociation around them. Easier, but less useful.

The slight double entendre of the previous paragraph was intentional: some of the things that bodies in therapy want to do to each other are indeed sexual. But the idea of sexual feelings is a good deal more prevalent than their actuality: in fantasy – often the fantasy of other people rather than the two participants – it can take over from all the many other impulses that will arise – to fight, to run away, to push and pull, to kick, to shake, to hold gently, to dance with, to tickle! Embodiment, sad to say, is often wholly identified with sexuality; this is one of the most stultifying aspects of our contemporary culture, and can make embodied therapy very difficult.

However it also gives therapy the task of opening out people's sense of bodily relationship to include more than sexuality: reminding them of the infinite sensuousness of embodied existence, the continuous relationship we build with the world through smell, taste, touch, sight and hearing, along with other more subtle sensory pathways like kinaesthesia and proprioception. Embodied therapy invites clients to play with their bodily experience, to flirt with the sensory universe. Again with the double entendre! – because we can't open our bodily senses without addressing the sexual framing of bodily experience which stands in the way.

This sexualisation of the senses is equivalent to what Ferenczi (1933/1999) called the 'confusion of tongues' between child and adult ways of being in the world. It is possible to have what we can call an erotic relationship with being alive, a constant renewal of joy and pleasure in existence, which in some ways is founded very literally on the physical act of breathing, the sensation of the breath moving down into and back up from our pelvis. Many children live wholly or partly in this state of erotic aliveness.

As we grow up in Western culture, this erotic quality tends to become increasingly restricted to sexuality, and genital sexuality at that: our genitals are a sort of indigenous reservation where the erotic charge that is taboo elsewhere in life is allowed to make its home. Therapy which supports clients in exploring their embodied experience is bound to connect both with the taboo pleasure of embodied aliveness, and with the pain of loss that attaches to it. This is particularly intense when the focus is on embodied relationship.

Embodied relating is by far the most interesting and challenging aspect of embodied therapy. Useful and important as it is to help clients explore their internally focused bodily experience, there comes a point sooner or later when the energy flows into impulses that relate to the other – specifically, the therapist. They begin to feel an embodied urge to do something to us. As soon as this urge starts to flicker into existence, I try to support it and respond to it, gently enough that I don't scare it away.

Often the first impulses are to fend me off, just as on a verbal and fantasy level the first transference feelings are often resistance: the client wants to push me away, to turn aside from me, to jostle me and tussle with me. As we physically explore these interactions, they may develop into a scenario of defiance and standing one's ground; once the client has experienced their own power to say 'No' to me, the desire and capacity for a more interactive physicality may develop, an exploration of how our bodies can cooperate and play with each other.

Strong feelings of love or attraction in the therapy room are often experienced as scary and disruptive. In training and supervision erotic feelings are sometimes not explored, or else the emphasis is on suppressing them (cf. Mann, 1997: Ch 2). Yet they are a very frequent part of therapy, and, I suggest, an inevitable accompaniment of the intimacy and intensity of the relationship and the encouragement it offers to surrender to spontaneity. More than that, erotic charge can be a powerful tool for therapeutic change. But I hope I have made clear in this talk that *eros* is only a part, though a very important part, of therapeutic intimacy. What I most want to communicate is my belief that therapeutic intimacy is something unique, which needs thinking about in its own terms and not simply translating into the more familiar languages of sexual relationship, child–child, or child–parent.

9

An Extraordinary Ordinariness

Nangaku picked up a tile and started to polish it. Baso, his disciple, asked 'What are you doing?' 'I want to make this tile into a jewel,' Nangaku said. 'How is it possible to make a tile a jewel?' Baso asked. 'How is it possible to become a Buddha by practicing zazen?' Nangaku replied. 'Do you want to attain Buddhahood? There is no Buddhahood besides your ordinary mind.'

(Shunryu Suzuki, *Zen Mind, Beginner's Mind*)

This is not really the time for an argument. Peter Lomas has died, and these papers are brought together to celebrate his life and achievement, which all the authors believe to be considerable. I agree with them: Lomas was an important figure for the alternative history of psychotherapy in the UK and beyond, someone who articulated a coherent position which took issue both with the symptom-focused, evidence-based rigidity of much contemporary therapy and counselling, and with the abstract house of cards erected by the more intellectual versions of psychoanalysis. He was one of the first to emphasise the crucial role of the therapeutic relationship; and also an early opponent of the regulation of psychotherapy, which he described as 'an exercise in public relations' (Lomas, 1999: 136) applying 'criteria of excellence ... that are abysmally inappropriate to psychotherapy', with disastrous consequences for our work (Lomas, 1999: 134; Lomas was referring not to state regulation, which had not yet been initiated, but to regulation by the psychotherapy and counselling organisations themselves).

Peter Lomas was also clearly a wonderful person to know: I only met him once myself, but his warmth and humanity were clear in that encounter, and emerge vividly from the papers under consideration. One thing I remember him saying which is not really brought out in these papers is that, although his history tied him to

---

2011. Written for the *European Journal of Psychotherapy and Counselling* as a response to articles in a special issue in memory of Peter Lomas, who died in 2010.

the psychoanalytic label, he now felt that really the title 'humanistic psychotherapist' best represented how he worked.

This is not the time for an argument – although they happen at many of the best wakes. It is not inappropriate, however, to explore whether the accounts of his thinking which these papers offer are open to question. Everyone has their own version of someone like Peter Lomas, possibly the more so the closer they are to him; and to some extent all these authors create Lomas afresh in terms of their own concerns and preoccupations – generally not dissimilar to his, but perhaps still not identical. This is most problematic in areas where Lomas's own thinking is arguably unclear or unconvincing.

I am thinking of two themes in particular: ordinary language, and the role of values in therapy. Both of these are very important in Lomas's work, where his account is subtle and highly nuanced. It seems to me that the versions of his ideas which appear in these papers are a lot less subtle and nuanced, and in some cases just plain wrong. Some of this wrongness may in fact be Lomas's; we need to do some unpacking in order to form a judgement.

The theme of ordinary language comes up in all the papers under consideration. John Heaton's paper (Heaton, 2011) is actually entitled 'The Ordinary', and centres entirely on the question of ordinary language. Heaton pathologises the use of difficult language and novel terminology, seeing it as the product of a need to feel 'special'. He accepts that special language is required for 'subjects we are not ordinarily familiar with' (Heaton, 2011: 50); but – rather extraordinarily in my view – he does not include psychotherapy within this category.

Though concerned also with further issues, the other papers all at least mention the theme of ordinary language. Sian Morgan describes Lomas as writing 'so clearly, concisely and without pretention' (Morgan, 2011: 18). Stephen Logan suggests that while, in the world of psychotherapy, 'there are other writers who seem cleverer, more learned, more prolific in teasing paradox and suggestive epigram, more allusive, knottier, promisingly obscure and of course more ostentatiously sophisticated', Lomas, in contrast, 'had the intelligence to know that cleverness is often a poor substitute for intelligence. I suspect he habitually subdued any impulse in himself to make a parade of his learning, or his capacity for ingenious interpretation, because he valued something else more' (this passage was cut from the published version of the paper, but not from my response). Paul Gordon enlists Lomas in the cause of writing with 'no postmodern tricksiness, no literary showing off, no brain-deadening jargon' (Gordon, 2011: 25); he suggests that for Lomas, therapy is 'something ordinary that was best captured in ordinary language' (ibid).

It seems to me that there are three different ideas about ordinariness involved here. One is that therapy is an ordinary activity; another is that it is best conducted in ordinary language; and the third is that it is best written about in ordinary language. None of these positions either depends on or leads to the other two; and each requires careful consideration.

If therapy is an ordinary activity, this can surely only be in a very special sense! For two people to make an appointment to regularly spend an hour together alone in a room, using this time mainly for one person to talk, but often with long periods of silence, and with the other person concentrating deeply, 'with rigorous care and thought' (Lomas, 1999: 7), on the implications and significances of the first person's speech – all this is certainly highly unusual in our society; to call it 'ordinary' must be to use the word to mean something other than 'common', 'normal', 'everyday'. And to write or talk about such an interaction is to address, in John Heaton's words, something 'we are not ordinarily familiar with' (Heaton, 2011: 50), requiring us to mint new terms and new ideas.

It is not my experience either that therapy, once it is well under way, is conducted in ordinary language. Most of the words used will, it is true, be individually familiar ones. But through what Sian Morgan nicely calls the 'passionate exchange' of the therapy relationship (Morgan, 2011: 15), these ordinary words are melted down and reforged, fused together and newly organised into meanings that are often completely unique to this particular relationship – meanings, it sometimes feels, that have never quite existed at all before this relationship came into being (Chapters 6 and 15, this volume).

Peter Lomas writes at length in all his books about ordinariness, including the ordinariness of the therapy relationship. Reading these papers sent me back, as of course it should, to reread Lomas; and it seems to me that he is quite intentionally using paradox in what he says about ordinariness. What needs to be 'ordinary' about therapy, he suggests, is actually something highly unusual: what he describes in *Cultivating Intuition* as 'an attempt, on both sides, to make a relationship' in which the therapist must 'not be content with interpreting the defences which stand in the way of intimacy, nor even with adopting a receptive stance to the patient, but ... should take the responsibility of getting to know him or her' (Lomas, 1974/1994: 133).

The whole point of this passage is that such an approach is in Lomas's view not at all 'ordinary' for therapists (he is writing at this point from psychoanalytic assumptions – such an approach was always more familiar in humanistic circles). It has become somewhat more so since 1994, when this was published, because of what is often called 'the relational turn' in psychoanalysis and psychotherapy; and Lomas should be given much more credit as a pioneer of this approach. But also – and Lomas certainly recognises this – such a relationship is for many people not part of their ordinary experience in life; and in fact the absence of such relating, both in childhood and currently, is precisely what brings many people to therapy. In this and many other passages about 'ordinariness' and 'naturalness', Lomas is subtly playing with the complex relationship between what is *natural* and what is *usual*, in the same sort of way that Zen masters describe (in far from ordinary language) being 'ordinary' as the highest human achievement (Suzuki, 1973).

It is all too easy, though, to collapse the paradox and drain the subtlety out of the discussion of ordinariness, reducing it to a reverse-snobbery attack on highfalutin' intellectuals who make a fuss about nothing; and I suggest that there is a tendency in this direction in the papers under consideration. I want to return now to the notion that therapy should be discussed, rather than conducted, in ordinary language. The question that immediately arises is: *whose* ordinary language? What is ordinary for one person is extremely strange to someone else; the ordinary language of academic papers like these, and the language I am using to write about them, is not ordinary at all in many ordinary contexts – in fact, let's face it, only a very small percentage of the population could make sense of what we are talking about. Take John Heaton's argument for the rejection of specialised language for discussing psychotherapy:

> Our ordinary, 'home-spun' languages have developed a subtle vocabulary for describing feelings, emotions, thoughts, desires, etc. This language has developed over thousands of years and been crafted in the living together of people in the society which uses the language. We are all intimate with our particular 'mother tongue' which we have been exposed to from birth; we have used it to express ourselves to others, and others have used it to express themselves about us. We are intimate with it because it was crafted in intimacy; special languages are not.
> (Heaton, 2011: 50)

This passage is not itself written in ordinary, 'home-spun' language, because such language did not evolve to discuss language itself and the ways in which it is used. In order to use meta-levels of

An Extraordinary Ordinariness 55

meaning – even more so in order to *discuss* meta-levels of meaning – we necessarily have to leave the terrain of everyday speech. This is amusingly demonstrated in Heaton's next paragraph, where he explains that 'ordinary language is permeated by ambiguity, polysemy, compression of meaning, subtlety and plurality of interpretation, rhetorical tropes, etc' (Heaton, 2011: 50). How many users of 'ordinary language' would understand that sentence?

The simple fact is that what each person experiences as 'ordinary language' is language with which they themselves happen to be comfortable, through education and background, and also as a function of individual personality. I am not certain how fully Lomas himself was aware of the relativity of ordinariness, but it is demonstrated in his own writing. Take the following passage from *The Limits of Interpretation*, quoted by Sian Morgan:

> If there has been a failure of holding, the child may manifest intolerable anxiety, with the consequence that the parent may overprotect her. The child's confidence as a viable entity will thereby be dimmed; she will believe it necessary to seek protection and a vicious circle will develop. In this case it is extraordinarily difficult to disentangle true need from induced need for a protectiveness that only stifles ... The therapist who wishes to counteract these kinds of traumatic experiences has to adopt a different stance in each case and to make a distinction between deprivation (not enough holding) and the impingement on the self which is a consequence of overprotectiveness ... Holding is only therapeutic if the basic anxiety has been faced. A desperate search for holding may be instigated by someone who uses the support as a distraction to avoid true insight. In this case apparent growth may occur, but it merely confirms the patient's addiction to an artificial intensity of experience.
> (Lomas, 1987: 86)

This is certainly, to use Morgan's earlier phrase, clear, concise and unpretentious. But could we really call it ordinary? It draws deeply on, and makes good use of, the whole intellectual tradition of psychoanalysis. It is clear to other people familiar with that tradition – so much so that it may be hard for us to see its strangeness; but even to other well-read and well-educated people who know nothing much about psychoanalysis, it will surely be very hard to grasp, and to those less educated, clear as mud. This is all the more so because many (though not all) of the words used are relatively common ones – but used with a specialised, technical twist into which the reader needs to be initiated. (It is also worth pointing out the use of 'she' rather than 'he' as a generic pronoun – a piece of non-ordinary language with a very clear and deliberate purpose.)

I do not myself see this strangeness as any sort of problem, but as an inevitable aspect of trying to write about subtle and complex psychological experiences which have not been widely considered outside the world of therapy. It is no more problematic than for a physicist to write in specialised terms about physics, or a sports writer about football. But this does seem to be a problem for Heaton and Gordon, at least, among the authors of these papers; apparently because their own preference is for writing about therapy in a different specialised language, one which Lomas himself came gradually to prefer: the language of values, morality and ethics.

We should note that this language is really no less 'special' than the technical language of psychotherapy, though it perhaps looks more 'ordinary' (I think these inverted commas have been earned by now). John Heaton points out (2011: 51) that mental mechanisms, unlike those of a watch, cannot be perceived or measured; but he seems unworried that the same is true of souls, love and goodness – in fact it is true of very many of the most important aspects of our experience. But because talking about love, for example, *sounds* ordinary, we are tempted to assume that we know what 'love' means and not to ask enough questions about how the other person is using it. One of the great advantages of non-ordinary language is that it is less subject to this assumption of shared understanding; on the other hand, this may be one of the things about it that alienates some people.

Lomas became increasingly clear over the course of his career that therapy is, in Paul Gordon's words, 'inevitably bound up with the ethical, that therapy is, sooner or later, about moral choices, about how to live' (Gordon, 2011: 26). But he was also very strongly aware that this position itself lays us open to ethical pitfalls. How are we to have a genuine interaction with our clients around moral choices about how to live without seeking to influence their choices in ways which are actually unethical? I have myself written several times (e.g. Chapters 14 and 15, this volume) about the impossibility of conducting therapy without having a position on how people should live, and about the importance of not pretending otherwise. Lomas makes this point in *Doing Good?*:

> If the therapist ... denies that he has an emotion which the patient has sensed intuitively, the latter will become uncertain of the validity of his own perceptions ... Similarly, if the therapist, by omitting to respond, implies that his patient's

moral outlook is of no concern to him yet clearly abhors his blatant racism, a similar confusion can easily occur.

(Lomas, 1999: 49)

Too great a reticence around moral (I might say political) disclosure, in other words, is as potentially damaging as too great a reticence around emotional disclosure. But disclosure in and of itself does not solve the ethical problem. Lomas discusses at length the difficulty of the 'moral influence' which the therapist may exercise over their client (Lomas, 1999: Ch 4). I am not sure that Lomas manages to resolve the issue; but then I am not sure that it can be resolved. The issue of moral influence – which I would describe myself as the issue of power relations in the therapy room – is, I believe, central to therapy, and also insoluble within therapy. The best thing we can do as practitioners is openly to admit this, and openly to struggle with it in our work with our clients. This attitude is itself far from 'ordinary' in the everyday world; it is something which children in particular seldom experience from adults, and this creates many of the wounds which people bring to therapy. I am quite sure that working with Peter Lomas as one's therapist would be very helpful in addressing such wounds.

These two questions, about ordinary language and about values, are very closely linked. The wish for ordinary language in therapy is partly motivated by an awareness that control over language is one important way in which people, including therapists, can exercise undue power and impose their values on others. At the same time, though, 'ordinary' language has its own coercive power, because it is able to make certain points of view – usually conservative or reactionary ones – appear obvious and inevitable. Developing non-ordinary language, including language which is non-ordinary in relation to therapeutic theory, is perhaps the only way to challenge this.

But if we talk to our clients in bizarre and unfathomable ways, they will be alienated and confused; and Lomas was highly sensitive to this. This is an important part of what he means by advocating 'ordinary language'. It seems to me that what we do in therapy at its best is to spend a great deal of time clarifying our understanding of what our clients mean by the words they use, and what we mean by the words we use; and that out of this, and in particular through powerful relational interactions which become points of reference for the work, we develop a mutual language which is unique almost in the way that the language of twins is unique, and which offers a unique possibility of saying the things that this particular client and therapist need to say to each other.

I was excited to discover from Stephen Logan's paper (Logan, 2011: 34–5) that Lomas was working when he died on a book called *Natural Psychotherapy*. I have myself just finished a book called *Wild Therapy* (Totton, 2011c), which I gather addresses some of the same issues, and which exploits a similar ambiguity in its title. 'Wild' and 'natural' both apply equally to the human and the other-than-human worlds, in different ways, and this allows each word to be used as a lever to open up important questions about how we should live.

From Logan's account, it seems as though Lomas was writing about what I have come to call domestication: a process to which, since the Neolithic, we have subjected not only other species but also ourselves. We have paid a terrible price for this, a price which now seems likely to include much of the biosphere; and psychotherapy, at least as practised by someone like Lomas, is one of the few forces in our society able to counter human domestication at a level deep enough to be meaningful.

Where I part company with Logan – and I am not sure whether this also means parting company with Lomas – is when he argues that we refer to 'the organisation of the natural world' by 'the more scientific-sounding name of "ecology"' only in order 'to confer respectability on this interest' (Logan, 2011: 36). It is hard not to read this as a confession of profound ignorance about what 'ecology' means. I am convinced that if Peter Lomas knew, as he may have done, what an ecosystem is and how it works, he would have been profoundly moved and delighted by the knowledge, and would immediately grasp its relevance to psychotherapy. Like psychotherapy, at least as practised by Lomas and people like him, ecology shows us that self-regulation and mutuality are the most natural things in the world, that the world in fact depends on them for its existence. So the rejection of this term and this knowledge, apparently simply because of its unfamiliarity, is a very powerful example of the misuse of 'ordinariness' as a value which I have been trying to address throughout this paper.

I have tried to show what I find most important and valuable about Peter Lomas's ideas. I have done this in critical dialogue with the authors represented in this issue, because it seems to me that in some instances they have oversimplified and to a degree misrepresented Lomas's work, and made him appear less interesting than he actually is. I hope that my responses have not caused offense. They are a direct expression of my enormous respect for Lomas, and my wish that he be understood as the exceptional figure that I believe him to be. I was very chuffed to read in Sian Morgan's piece about the sticker on Lomas's car, 'I'm for Wild

Life' (Morgan, 2011: 13). It is Lomas's wildness, and the trickster quality that goes along with it, which I think is in danger of being lost in his representation as an apostle of too ordinary a kind of ordinariness.

10

Both/And

The first thing is to be clear about what pluralism isn't. On the one hand, pluralism is not schoolism: it in no way resembles the self-satisfied, 'neutral' listing of respectable modalities and their identifying characteristics. On the other hand, though, pluralism is not generic psychotherapy: it does not support the view, increasingly widespread these days, that there is a baseline, normative activity of psychotherapy which can be extracted from all the different schools and which transcends the differences between them.

One of the most important facts which we know about therapy – one of the few facts we know, I am tempted to say – is that the practitioner's modality makes little difference to the outcome of the work. With some minor qualifications, pretty much all the research agrees on this (e.g. Cooper, 2008: Ch 3; Roth & Fonagy, 1996: 341–57; Seligman, 1995). Whatever my practice, whether analytic, humanistic, integrative, cognitive, or something else, its success (as measured by client satisfaction – see below for a discussion of 'success') depends considerably on how the client perceives our relationship, how far they experience me as supportive and to be trusted (Roth & Fonagy, 1996: 350–5).

I suggest that the importance of this fact is often underestimated, and even more often misunderstood. The main misunderstanding is to conclude that it supports the notion of generic psychotherapy – that we are all doing much the same thing, and that it makes little difference which form of psychotherapy is chosen. There is a simple error of reasoning at work here. That several procedures have similar rates of success in no way implies that they are interchangeable.

The fact that the practitioner's modality makes little difference to the outcome does not mean that it makes little difference which modality we use (although it might give us the confidence to experiment). For a start, it makes a difference *to the practitioner*:

This one is a bit of a puzzle: to the best of my recollection it was written for a special issue of *The Psychologist* on pluralism. However, no such issue ever appeared, and I do not know whether the article has ever been published. If anyone knows, please inform me.

we all, hopefully, choose to train in modalities which suit our character, rather than modalities which would make us uncomfortable and inauthentic. Equally, to a considerable extent, at least in private practice, clients self-select a modality which appeals to them and which they feel capable of carrying through. People are different, and they need different sorts of therapy, both as clients and as practitioners.

The name of 'psychotherapy' is used by a tremendous range of significantly different activities. It would take a truly complex Venn diagram to map them. On a large number of meaningful axes, there is a clump of overlapping and similar practices around the middle, and a few mavericks off in the long grass at each end; and these mavericks are not the same for each axis. It is only through a set of historical accidents that all these activities have ended up being called 'psychotherapy'. Sometimes the differences of viewpoint are so large that the definitions of 'successful outcome' used by each therapy make comparative measurement impossible. The great tactical triumph of cognitive therapy has been to establish its own definition of therapeutic success, compatible with the 'objective' criteria measured in double-blind tests, as a norm against which all forms of therapy are measured. This is both absurd and unjust.

But the truly astonishing range of difference in the field of psychotherapy is not a problem. Far from being a problem, it is a positive strength: offering the richness and diversity of a psychological rainforest, as opposed to the agribusiness prairie which some interest groups seem to be trying to create (Postle, 1998). It reflects, in fact, the richness and diversity of our inner world, which cannot be reduced to any one system or methodology. Each form of psychotherapy has come into existence to express a further facet of the inexhaustible complexity of the psyche. Every form is 'true'; every form is partial.

Pluralism doesn't just recognise difference; it celebrates it. But also, as Andrew Samuels has been telling us for years (e.g. Samuels, 1997/2011, 2001), pluralism is not a postmodernist bogeyman. It asks of us simply that *we take our own side* – while simultaneously recognising that our own side is just that, the place where we are standing (at the moment), and trusting that by everyone taking their own side, representing their own position, the collective good will tend to be furthered. As psychotherapists we should be quite skilled at this: it is the basis on which most sorts of group therapy function, what Arnold Mindell (1992) calls 'deep democracy'.

In other words (Samuels again), pluralism is about a free market. 'The trademark of pluralism is competition and its way of life is bargaining' (Samuels, 1997/2011: 223). And one can legitimately ask of anything that seeks to regulate the free market: in whose interests is this being done? Is this regulation to ensure a level playing field, or to enforce a consistent slope?

Pluralism, then, is both an appropriate response to the actual state of psychotherapy, and an expression of what psychotherapy teaches us about negotiating difference. More than that: it is, perhaps, psychotherapy's best gift to the world, its major political contribution – a way to negotiate the baffling and enraging differences between cultures and societies which so strongly threaten our survival. 'Both/And' may not be a catchy slogan, but it is the one we need, both inside and outside psychotherapy.

11

Boundaries and Boundlessness

The inability to tolerate empty space limits the amount of space available.

(Wilfred Bion, 1992, *Cogitations*)

There is a quietly ferocious struggle going on for the soul of psychotherapy and counselling, manifesting in many ways – regulation, training, evidence-based practice – but ultimately about the tension between spontaneity and control. I want to examine how this tension operates in clinical practice, and in particular the ways in which a self-censorship or 'therapy police' is installed in practitioners – primarily through an insufficiently examined notion of boundaries.

Many supervisors have noticed how supervisees inhibit their own responses, and in fact their own best judgement, in line with an internal modelling of what they believe is expected of them by their profession. This is natural enough, and in some ways appropriate, for trainees or newly qualified practitioners who need to develop an 'internal supervisor', though even here it can be unhelpfully exaggerated; but for experienced therapists or counsellors it acts as a block to authentic relationship with their clients, founded on a sense of their own professional inadequacy.

Joseph Sandler, an elder of psychoanalysis, wrote in 1983 that 'the conviction of many analysts [is] that they do not do "proper" analysis ... that what is actually done in the analytic consulting room is not "kosher", that colleagues would criticize it if they knew about it' (Sandler, 1983: 38). He goes on to say:

> Any analyst worth his salt will adapt to specific patients on the basis of his interaction with those patients. He will modify his approach so that he can get as good as possible a working

---

2010. The publication of this piece in *Therapy Today* produced a large postbag, some supportive and some furious. I was accused of many things. However several workshops and talks on the topic have been enthusiastically attended. Boundaries and boundlessness became an important theme in my book *Wild Therapy* (2011c).

analytic situation developing. I believe that the many adjustments one makes in one's analytic work ... often lead to or reflect a better fit of the analyst's developing intrinsic private preconscious theory with the material of the patient than the official public theories to which the analyst may consciously subscribe.

(Sandler, 1983: 38)

Sandler is pointing out that in reality we spend a lot of our time flying by the seat of our pants, as it were – relying on our 'educated instincts' to shape our response, rather than taking time out to consult the rulebook. There are aspects of the training and culture of therapy, though, which militate against these 'adaptations and adjustments', or at any rate make the practitioner guilty and secretive about them. Gifted and well-established – and courageous – practitioners may be able to speak openly about how they have stepped outside the conventional framework – as when Brian Thorne writes about working naked with a client (Thorne, 1987), or Peter Lomas about taking a session out of doors (Lomas, 1974/1994: 146), or Mario Jacoby about physical contact with a client (M Jacoby, 1986) – but they are partially protected by the exceptionalism which attaches to celebrity: 'It's all right for *them*'. And even therapeutic celebrities have kept silent about some of their actions; Winnicott, for example, never revealed that he too touched some of his clients (Little, 1990). Indeed, one should note that Brian Thorne's account was resurrected and held up to scandal over 20 years later as a way of discrediting his opposition to state regulation of psychotherapy and counselling (Newman, 2010).

Beginning with Freud, though – as we can see from his clients' narratives collected in Lohser and Newton (1996) – it is clear that the therapy world operates on the principle 'Do what I say, not what I do', with many senior figures using a much more spontaneous and relational way of working themselves than they are willing to recommend to others. I have more than once had the experience, when speaking at a conference about my use of touch in therapy, of being told privately by some elderly and experienced figure: 'Well, I'm happy for you to work in this way, I can see you know what you're doing, and I might do some of it myself – but I would never publicly condone it.'

Touch is a useful example, because it so clearly constellates anxieties about 'wild' and out-of-control feelings and behaviour. These anxieties – both within the therapy profession and in the wider society – have intensified over recent decades, and become condensed into the quintessentially domesticated concept of 'appropriate therapeutic boundaries'. One thing that most newly qualified counsellors and psychotherapists are clear about is the importance of therapeutic boundaries. They may not necessarily be very good at maintaining them, but they know that doing so is essential. Unfortunately, this 'knowledge' is untrue, or at any rate incomplete.

Relatively new practitioners are so familiar with the notion of boundaries that it may come as quite a surprise to find out how recently it was introduced. A literature search shows that before the 1990s, therapists did not really speak of 'boundaries' in this specific sense, meaning 'lines of behaviour which must not be crossed, by the therapist, by the client, or both'. Of course issues of acceptable behaviour were discussed long before then, but under a variety of different headings; and there is something very significant about the way in which all these themes were gathered together under a single rubric which seems to have been borrowed originally from the discourse of sexual abuse.

The theory of boundaries which has grown up around work with survivors of sexual abuse is enormously helpful and clarifying – *within that context*. But its appropriation as a way of thinking about issues like fees, telephone contact or session times has had the effect of installing a subliminal notion of what both its advocates (e.g. Simon, 1989) and its opponents (e.g. Zur, 2004) have called the 'slippery slope' theory: that any flexibility or inventiveness around the usual ways of doing therapy – a single toke on the spliff of adaptability, so to speak – leads to the hard stuff, to sexual abuse of clients. It has been claimed in all seriousness by proponents of the 'slippery slope' theory – writing not in the 1920s but in the 1990s – that the use of first names between practitioner and client is a predictor of sexual abuse further down the line (Epstein & Simon, 1990; Gutheil & Gabbard, 1993).

Freud is very often blamed for this state of affairs, because of the technical papers on psychoanalysis which he wrote to guide young practitioners (Freud, 1912, 1913, etc.). Whatever one feels about his recommendations (which is explicitly what they were), it is interesting to find that Freud very often quite openly frames them not as a protection for the *analysand*, but as for the benefit or convenience of the *practitioner*.

> The psycho-analyst who is asked to undertake the treatment of the wife or child of a friend must be prepared for it to cost him [sic] that friendship, no matter what the outcome of the treatment may be: nevertheless he must make the sacrifice if he cannot find a trustworthy substitute.
> (Freud, 1913: 125)

And a little later in the same paper:

> [H]e should also refrain from giving treatment free, and make no exceptions to this in favour of his colleagues or their families. This last recommendation will seem to offend against professional amenities. It must be remembered, however, that a gratuitous treatment means much more to a psycho-analyst than to any other medical man; it means the sacrifice of a considerable portion – an eighth or a seventh part, perhaps – of the working time available to him for earning his living, over a period of many months.
>
> (Freud, 1913: 132)

Freud is mainly thinking practically, flexibly, locally; he might have been quite surprised to find Robert Langs (e.g. 1998) arguing that these local arrangements match the unconscious needs of *every single patient*. Langs' follower David L Smith lists a set of 21 'fundamental ground rules' including such matters as a set time, a set fee, and no gifts being accepted, which he claims all psychotherapy clients 'unconsciously want their therapists to follow irrespective of their conscious preferences. They appear to be *universal* rules' (Smith, 1991: 139). In a note he continues, ludicrously but quite logically, 'this implies that patients' unconscious secured-frame criteria are the product of hominid evolution' (Smith, 1991: 140).

The idea that we have evolved as a species to require a set time and fee in therapy is not widely held; but it *is* now widely held that all clients at all times should be treated within the same set of boundaries. Over something like 20 years, the idea that boundaries are a key element in therapy has become more and more dominant, to the extent that for many practitioners it is now part of their conceptual wallpaper, an axiom which they have perhaps never questioned. The emphasis on boundaries has been read back into earlier therapeutic formulations, and is now understood as universally present. But is this really the case?

The humanistic therapies, and in a different sense behavioural therapy, developed partly in reaction to what was seen as the rigid structure of psychodynamic work. Humanistic therapy stresses the importance of offering warm, genuine contact; while behavioural therapists, at least originally, saw their work as avoiding all the apparatus of transference and projection and simply applying expert techniques, so that the relationship is one between equals, equivalent to that with one's accountant or architect: 'The resulting relationship is one in which I have felt quite comfortable having good friends as clients and good clients as friends' (Marquis, 1972: 48-9; cf. Lazarus, 1994).

But the developing concept of appropriate boundaries, and in particular its codification in legal and quasi-legal structures, increasingly forces all therapists and counsellors into *defensive practice* – that is, working in ways which are based not on giving the client the therapeutic environment best suited to them, but on avoiding vulnerability to misconduct hearings. In a crucial contribution to the theory of therapeutic boundaries, Gutheil and Gabbard (1993) developed a distinction between 'boundary violations', which they see as always harmful, and 'boundary crossings', which may be neutral or beneficial. However, they also argued that even boundary crossings which are justified and consistent with good care should be avoided, on the basis of their possible adverse appearance in court. This process of avoiding behaviours not because they are wrong, but only because they *appear* wrong, is known as 'risk management'.

According to Gutheil and Gabbard, 'the risk-management value of avoiding even the appearance of boundary violations should be self-evident'. But there are other values central to therapy that may occasionally demand 'the *appearance* of boundary violations', or at least certainly that we do not *'avoid'* that appearance. Therapy is as much about questioning boundaries as it is about asserting them; as much about supporting clients to break out of the rules as it is about teaching them to observe the rules. For some clients at some times, it is crucial to know that the therapist will act within a defined frame. For others, or for the same clients at other times, it is equally crucial that the therapist dances outside the frame, and that a trust can be established which is based on authenticity rather than on predictability.

Therapy based on authenticity may reasonably be characterised as 'undefensive practice', as opposed to the 'defensive practice' which is becoming more and more the norm of contemporary therapy. Undefensive practitioners are vulnerable to misunderstanding, and indeed, if not sufficiently self-monitoring, to misbehaviour; but defensive practitioners, in the extreme, neither like nor trust their clients – they see them as a potential threat, a danger to be negotiated. On one level this threat is to the practitioner's standing and income, should a complaint be made; but more deeply, one feels that the real threat is to the practitioner's insecure self-image and self-esteem. Their internal critic is projected out into their clients, who are then mistrusted and feared.

A more positive and realistic picture of the situation is put forward by Johnston and Farber (1996), who surveyed what practitioners think and do around 'everyday' boundaries in psychotherapy – starting and ending sessions on time, payment of fees, changing session times, and so on. They found that:

> Patients make relatively few demands and psychotherapists accommodate them most of the time. This finding stands in opposition to the generally accepted image of the psychotherapist standing firm in the face of persistent attempts by the patient to challenge existing boundaries and suggests a spirit of cooperation and good faith under emphasized in theoretical writings.
>
> (Johnston & Farber, 1996: 397)

Jodie Messler Davies (2004) describes the extreme difficulty of working, while having a heavy cold, with a client she refers to as Karen, who seems to use Davies's illness to confirm her negative picture of their relationship, and calls her 'such a bitch ... cold and unfeeling', leaving Davies 'stunned' (2004: 715). However (after some splendid self-supervision on Davies' part) something transformative happens in the next session:

> On Friday afternoon I am still sick ... I brace myself for Karen's entrance. ... But I notice, almost immediately, that something feels palpably different. The air feels warmer, her eyes look softer and more searching, my own body seems to relax even before I can formulate the experience.
> ...
> Karen reaches down into her book bag and pulls out a large silver thermos and mug. As she opens the thermos and begins to pour, the warm smells of honey, vanilla and cinnamon fill my office. I am mesmerized as I watch Karen, intrigued with her swift and competent movements. 'This will be good for you,' she says. 'My grandmother used to make it for me when I was sick. It is a combination of hot tea and hot milk with a lot of other wonderful stuff.'
>
> (Davies, 2004: 725)

At this point, alerted by CCTV, the Therapy Police smash down the door and storm into the consulting room. All of the familiar objections to 'gratifying' the client flash through Davies' mind, and all of the ways in which an 'interpretation' could maintain the therapist's control of the situation. 'I try to will myself to think, despite the feverish "buzz" in my head. My patient is attempting to feed me warm milk! There must be an incredible interpretation in this somewhere!' (Davies, 2004: 725). For paragraphs of text, though probably only a few microseconds of real time, she wrestles with her internal judges, with her intellectual process. Then she takes the milk.

She holds the mug out to me, an expression of intense pleasure and hopefulness suffusing her face. As I reach for the mug our fingers touch for an instant and I recall that my own grandmother brought a similar recipe with her from Russia; one she would prepare for us when someone in the family was sick with a cold.
...
I take Karen's mug in my own hands, breathing in its healing, aromatic warmth. ... the intoxicating smells and moist heat penetrate and soothe. ... I take a long, deep, healing gulp of Karen's milk ... I smile at Karen through the steam, and she smiles back.

(Davies, 2004: 725-7)

We can take this as an example of undefensive practice – informed and guided as of course it must be by a critical understanding of the many levels involved, but not *controlled* by that understanding The focus is a deeply embodied interaction. There is a lot about touch, taste, smell; Karen brings a 'palpably different' atmosphere when she arrives, the air feels warmer, her eyes softer, her smile warmer and evoking an answering smile from the therapist. The mug of milky tea, the 'wonderful stuff', is described in highly sensuous terms; as it is passed over, 'our fingers touch for an instant', and both client and therapist recall their grandmother. This is a multisensory, multidimensional, psychosomatic interaction, bringing with it an abundance of positive memories and associations for both people. It is a moment of healing.

Of course, it is only the beginning of a long process of coming to understand a very difficult relationship. But it seems clear that this undefensive embodied interaction, where so much is both communicated and expressed, through so many sensory channels, creates a bridge of intersubjectivity over which other communications can then pass. Embodied relationship, in fact, is 'wonderful stuff': the milk of human kindness! And sometimes we must take the risk that the milk *might* be poisoned, the client might be seeking to manipulate us in some way. The risk we take is the authentic expression of our wish for contact with the other.

Every therapeutic relationship needs to be a *relationship:* a place where two subjectivities meet, with all the difficulty and painfulness this implies, but also with a developing willingness and capacity to tolerate the other person's otherness. For a therapist to hold careful boundaries because they believe they *must,* or because they are afraid of the uncontrollability of closeness, cripples the potential for relatedness; but for a therapist to hold such boundaries as an honouring of the client's woundedness is itself relational. The only valid generalisation about relationships is that they are each unique; and therapists are artisans of relationship, co-creating one-off works with their clients.

What is the opposite of being boundaried? One answer is 'unboundaried'; another is 'boundless'. Undefensive practice, I suggest, draws on a sense of boundlessness – abundance, space, attention, care. In contact with abundance, the therapist can afford to be generous on many levels; which communicates the experience of abundance to the client, perhaps allowing them to relax about life and its challenges. Yes, a practitioner who cannot offer her clients boundaries is dangerous. But a practitioner who cannot offer her clients boundlessness is useless.

12

Not a Tame Lion: Psychotherapy in a safety-obsessed culture

'Is he – quite safe? I shall feel rather nervous about meeting a lion.' 'That you will, dearie, and make no mistake,' said Mrs. Beaver; 'if there's anyone who can appear before Aslan without their knees knocking, they're either braver than most or else just silly.' 'Then he isn't safe?' said Lucy. 'Safe?' said Mr. Beaver; 'don't you hear what Mrs. Beaver tells you? Who said anything about safe? 'Course he isn't safe. But he's good.'

(CS Lewis, *The Lion, the Witch and the Wardrobe*)

Unlike Aslan, therapy is definitely not God; but there are some parallels. The thesis of this chapter will be that if therapy is going to be good, it can't also be safe.

By 'good', I mean tending to increase the range of clients' relaxation, freedom, expression and self-acceptance; by 'safe', I mean free from pain, anxiety and risk of failure. But there are some very different understandings of 'good' and 'safe' currently circulating in the therapy world, and this is part of what I want to write about. Some schools of thought understand 'good' to mean capable of swiftly alleviating presenting symptoms, and 'safe' to mean defensive practice which ticks appropriate precautionary boxes. I think that the main line of development of psychotherapy and counselling cannot be fitted into this second model, and that attempts to do so are deeply problematic.

One of the messages of psychotherapy and counselling – hereinafter known as 'therapy' – has always been: 'Relax, nothing is under control (and that's OK)'. Therapy has stood against the dominant cultural message, 'Be in control of yourself and your environment': it has tried to help people tolerate the anxiety of not being in control – of our feelings, our thoughts, our body, our future.

2011. A chapter contributed to *Towards Professional Wisdom: Practical Deliberations in the People Professions* [Bondi et al, 2011], and in some ways my favourite of my several treatments of these issues. This version removes some material covered in other chapters, and includes part of a talk entitled 'Therapy has no goal: a radical model of practice' given at the BACP Annual Conference, 2008, which helps to clarify some of my points.

Some classic texts on this are Freud (1926b), Reich (1942/1973 and 1933/1975), Fromm (1942/1960), Winnicott (1949/1992), Rogers (1978), Berne (1968), and Perls, Hefferline & Goodman (1951/1973); there are many others.

There has always been a tussle over this issue, however: new methods constantly arise – Redecision Therapy, Neurolinguistic Programming, Cognitive Behavioural Therapy, Eye Movement Desensitization and Reprocessing – which make the comforting claim 'You *can* be in control after all: you can choose your emotions and live according to your conscious will'. This is far more acceptable to the dominant social structure, which now also says that therapy itself must be controlled, brought within the field of regulation. This is one aspect of a general trend towards ever-widening regulation: as the world becomes increasingly frightening, it becomes increasingly necessary to claim that security *can* be achieved, through monitoring, surveillance and censorship. This is the path our society is taking; but equally, it is an *internal,* psychological process, embracing exactly the anxieties which therapy arose to address.

From a psychological point of view, this path of control is in effect a project to eliminate the unconscious. 'Aslan' actually represents in this chapter not God, not therapy, but what I believe to be therapy's true subject, the unconscious, that aspect of our bodymind which is beyond all control. And the social project of regulation and surveillance is closely parallel to that of the White Witch and her Secret Police Chief Maugrim, who forbid all acknowledgement of Aslan's existence. But when the repressed returns to Narnia, the snow melts, flowers spring up, and everyone who has been turned to stone is restored to life. Not a safe process! – But a good one.

If Aslan is not a tame lion, then he is a wild lion. Therapy can often be terribly tame; but in my view it is essentially wild, a focus of resistance to compulsory human domestication. This is the context for what follows.

Not knowing

> Acceptance of not-knowing produces tremendous relief.
> (DW Winnicott, 1949/1992: 250)

What perhaps makes psychotherapy truly valuable, beyond all the interpretations and adjustments, is that it can offer a space free of goals and intentions. Goals, however benign, tend to carry with them a demand for their achievement; and demands are what we suffer from, a suffering which brings us into therapy in the first place, and which therapy can potentially alleviate. This is paradoxical, since freeing us from demands is itself a goal, and therefore carries a demand from which the therapeutic space must in turn be freed – which becomes a further demand, and so on .... But a tolerance of, even an insistence on, paradox is perhaps one of the features which make therapy, like other techniques of liberation, not a tame lion.

Let me start, though, by addressing a probably largely imaginary audience: people who follow my work year by year, and who *demand* from me (notice the word) a basic consistency of discourse. If there are any such readers here, they will be wondering how I can reconcile the argument I am making now with my often-expressed view (see Chapters 15 and 16) that therapy always takes a position, explicit or implicit, on *how people should be*. You may be wondering this; my internal critic certainly is.

And that allows me to make an instant demonstration of what I am saying about demands, and how they bring people to therapy. Unless we are sociopaths, we all suffer from our internal critics: from a set of essentially imaginary requirements that we be a certain way, achieve certain standards, meet certain criteria. Witnessing your own process you may have noticed that there is a built-in impossibility about these demands, in that the goalposts are constantly moving. It's rather like accreditation: as soon as you think you're almost there, the target recedes in front of you. Our internal critic doesn't actually *care* about our efforts to meet its demands. Its function is to attack us for failing to do so.

In this instance I have an answer to my internal/imaginary critic about the apparent inconsistency between my two positions, that therapy has no goals, and that therapists always take a view on how people should be. The point is not that therapists *should* take such a view; or that they shouldn't. We do it because this is something that human beings do, just as we live in groups, adorn our bodies, and assess each other's relative status. It's no more use arguing with this sort of trait than it is arguing with the weather. What is useful and important is bringing awareness to our own positions as we deploy them in the therapy room, and bringing awareness to our clients' responses.

Notice also the distinction between *therapists* and *therapy*. Therapeutic practice, from one point of view, is an ongoing struggle by the therapist to live up to the aspirations of therapy – to become aware of and release the biases and fantasies which lead us to demand, implicitly, that the client and reality be a certain way. This ongoing practice of awareness and release is why and how being a therapist, as well as hopefully being good for clients, is good for *us*. But another paradox of therapy is that it can only be good for anybody when it confronts and gives up its *intention* to be good for them. This is a corollary of the paradoxical theory of change (Beisser, 1972): not only does change happen when the client stops trying to change – it happens when the therapist stops trying to change them.

Therapists' demands on the client express what Lynne Layton (2004, 2006) calls the 'normative unconscious', our internalisation of social norms. As Perls et al (along with many others) point out, 'Our society frequently demands the impossible of us. ... Since such demands are so insistently and universally pressed upon us, we feel that they *must* make sense' (Perls, Hefferline & Goodman, 1951/1973: 108). These impossible demands are internalised, becoming sticks with which we constantly beat ourselves; out of these demands, and out of our resistance to them, we construct our identity.

According to Althusser (1971) identity is created through a process of 'interpellation', which can roughly be translated as 'hailing'– 'Hey, you!' If we are addressed repeatedly in certain ways, then we take on the identity which is ascribed to us, together with the requirements that attach to it. Maintaining this interpellated self becomes the source of tremendous anxiety and tension. As a body psychotherapist, I perceive this tension to be anchored in the voluntary musculature, as we habitually tighten our bodies to represent, and to resist, the 'self' which has been imposed on us; to resist, and to represent, the spontaneous impulses of the bodymind.

There are at least three levels to this interpellated self. One level is made up of the specific requirements of our family, its specific rules about which emotions can be expressed when, about what lifestyles and occupations are permissible, about whether and when we are allowed to enjoy ourselves, and so on. Also about our particular *role* in the family, scapegoat or hero, invalid or supermum. Then there is the level of our culture's demands on us – injunctions about gender, for example, about ambition, about aggression. But also there is the meta-demand which enjoins us to *be consistent*, to *stay the same*. As I listen to my clients and to my own internal monologue, I hear a lot of energy being expended on producing a consistent narrative, ironing out contradictions and ambiguities. But contradictions and ambiguities, for example feeling more than one thing at the same time, are a fundamental aspect of being human. Our friends and family very often police this injunction; you have probably noticed how little most people like it when we *change* noticeably, even when the change is plainly an improvement. And, of course, we police our friends and family in the same way: 'You're really different today, not like yourself!'

Clearly, therapists have every opportunity to reinforce interpellation, to 'hail' the client in ways that they are accustomed to, telling them that they are who they have always been told they are. We also have the opportunity to tell them that they are in fact someone else, someone new – someone who conforms better to *our own* picture of what people should be like. We can offer them a *new* consistent narrative. Not only can we do one or both of these things to our clients – they can do they same to us. But we also have a wonderful opportunity *not* to tell them who they are: neither to feed back the familiar picture, nor to create a new one, but rather to work 'without memory or desire', as WR Bion famously put it (Bion, 1967/1988: 18), allowing the familiar self gently to deconstruct and to loosen its grip on the bodymind. This involves a subtle and continuous exploration of transference and countertransference – the client's ways of 'recognising' us as the familiar interpellator/critic, and our ways of responding to this recognition.

Therapy thus understood is an *enlightenment practice*, paralleling other such other practices which occur within Buddhism, Hinduism, Islam, Taoism, Judaism, Christianity, and a few other settings. Not that therapy is identical or similar to any one of the above, any more than they are identical or similar to each other. But what I am calling 'enlightenment practices' have some features in common, which therapy – in at least some of its forms – shares, sufficiently so to be seen as another approach to the same task. Broadly speaking, the enlightenment practices all lead us to the sense that something which previously seemed hugely important and hugely difficult is now quite trivial. The relief which this entails is enormous and life changing.

Like other enlightenment practices, psychotherapy works by temporarily substituting its own 'impossible demands' for those which we experience in life in general. This can have the effect of bringing the client to a realisation that some of the other tasks which life seems to involve – for example, reparation, spontaneity, consistency – are impossible: that they are paradoxical, and finally meaningless. Each enlightenment practice has its own techniques for doing this. In Zen there are koans, for instance: unanswerable questions which one is required to answer, like 'What is the sound of one hand clapping?' In almost every tradition there is some form of meditation, where one is required to attend closely to one's spontaneous process without changing it.

In therapy, the original, classic technique which corresponds to these is free association, the demand that the client says everything which passes through their mind. This is a demand with which no one can fully comply; as Ferenczi first pointed out, it 'represents an ideal which ... can only be fulfilled after the analysis has ended' (Ferenczi, 1927/1999: 147). In other words, as Adam Phillips puts it, one is cured not *by* free association, but when one *can* free associate (Phillips, 1995: 102). I'm not actually sure that *anyone* can free associate; or rather that, while free associating, anyone can remain 'themselves', continuing to scan themselves for consistency.

One function of the demand to free associate, then, is to highlight its *impossibility*: to make us forcibly aware of our resistances and inhibitions – and, more deeply, of our lack of title, so to speak, in what is said, thought and felt: that the 'I' who is supposed to be the source and origin of our thoughts and words is in reality a fiction, an artefact. Very few therapists these days work explicitly with free association, which is perhaps a shame (the body psychotherapist's equivalent technique is breathwork); but many of us certainly put a steady, implicit pressure on clients to respond spontaneously and authentically, which is ultimately a generalised version of free association, and every bit as tricky to comply with – another form of paradoxical hailing.

The simple tactic of free association cuts deeply through our illusions, and single-handedly de-centres the ego: the impossibility of 'saying whatever comes into your head' reveals the impossibility of accounting for oneself, the impossibility of manifesting both consistency and spontaneity. We cannot *deliberately* be spontaneous, because we can never be anything else but spontaneous. The more we *try* to be spontaneous, the more stiff and anxious we get! – which of course doesn't mean that we are no longer spontaneous, just that we don't *feel* spontaneous. Equally, we feel inconsistent, because we imagine consistency as being a state in which everything is available to consciousness and fits together seamlessly. We also confuse this with authenticity. But there is no such state. The consistent thing about us is that we are in a process of continual and uneven change, so that different parts of us are occupying different positions. We tend to struggle desperately against this reality as we try to meet the demand for spontaneous authenticity which we experience in therapy.

If therapy succeeds in bringing enough non-critical awareness to this struggle, then the ego, which takes charge of our efforts to comply with such demands, is gradually seen to be only a figure of speech, a trick of the light – a state of bodily tension or of mental attention. The ego, in fact, is precisely, and is even nothing more than, the internalised demand for consistency; like a Polaroid camera which constantly takes photos to establish where we are. In Winnicott's terms, it is the 'mind', as something distinct from and in contradiction to the bodymind unity; he suggests that the experience of a mind/body opposition stems precisely from an experienced lack of steady, non-judgemental acceptance. 'In the overgrowth of the mental function reactive to erratic mothering, we see that there can develop an opposition between the mind and the psyche-soma' (Winnicott, 1949/1992: 246). A therapeutic space without goals, without demands, without interpellation – or rather, a space where these phenomena are noticed and deconstructed as they arise – may be able to heal this opposition and help what I call the 'spastic ego' to relax.

At this moment in the history of therapy, we are suffering from an increasingly dominant approach which thinks that 'effectiveness' is about the relief of symptoms. If I go to see a therapist because I am suffering from anxiety or obsession or insomnia, then it obviously makes crude sense to judge the effectiveness of the work in terms of how much this suffering has been alleviated by the time therapy ends. It is also what governments and insurance companies require. However, like most therapists, I often find that someone says when ending therapy, 'I still have my original symptom, but therapy has been a wonderful, life-changing process'. The person's *relationship* with their symptom has changed: it no longer stops them having a fulfilling life. This is what people often refer to as 'feeling better'; which is why that rather unscientific term is a crucial measurement of therapy's usefulness. It appears that all forms of therapy are pretty 'useful' to most people, perhaps especially long-term and relational approaches (Cooper, 2008; Seligman, 1995).

Expertise, local knowledge and thick description

I have quoted in Chapter 1 a fascinating complaint made in the early 1950s by the then President of the American Psychoanalytic Association. 'The great increase in numbers of trainees ... and ... the more structured training of institutes', he says, have changed the sort of people coming for training. In the glory days of the 1920s and early 1930s,

> many gifted individuals with definite neuroses or character disorders were trained. ... In contrast, perhaps the majority of students of the past decade or so have been 'normal' characters,

or perhaps one should say had 'normal character disorders'. They are not introspective, are inclined to read only the literature that is assigned in institute courses, and wish to get through with the training requirements as rapidly as possible. ... Their motivation for being analysed is more to get through this requirement of training rather than to ... explore introspectively and with curiosity their own inner selves.
(Knight, 1953: 218)

The result of this was a decade or more in which analysis in the USA became primarily a mechanism of social normalisation – until the human potential movement arose to oppose this. Something similar is happening now, again correlated with a huge expansion in practitioner numbers, leading to what Knight describes (ibid) as 'the partial capitulation of some institutes arising from numbers of students, from their ambitious haste, and from their tendency to be satisfied with a more superficial grasp of theory'. We are again in the age of the 'normal' practitioner.

In the same chapter, I connected this phenomenon with the re-medicalisation of therapy, and suggested that the rise of the 'normal practitioner' and the pressure for medicalisation entwine with a third factor: hunger for status. I described how powerful groups within therapy are seeking to repeat the success of medicine, responding to the need for a body of 'expert knowledge' by generating one – radically lengthening trainings, 'technicalising' every aspect of the work, inserting new levels and meta-levels of expertise and qualification so as to generate the expertise which is a requirement for every profession. This expertise:

> would have key characteristics: it would be taught in an organized way, most usually in a university (or at least in an institution that collects, transmits and eventually reproduces knowledge); and it would be standardized and accredited and often have scientific anchorage. ... Expert knowledge gives some the privilege to speak, to act as arbiters.
> (Cant & Sharma, 1996: 6)

The push for this has come from some influential and ambitious people in the therapy world; the pull has come from the 'normal trainees' wanting to be *told what to do*, and from a society which increasingly demands expertise before it will take anyone seriously. Only the vociferous opposition of large numbers of 'rank and file' practitioners has held regulation through the Health Professions Council at bay for so long.

In the same chapter (see also Chapters 2, 6 and 16), I argued that expertise occupies the opposite pole to *local knowledge* (Geertz, 1983), and that therapy is a classic example of the latter. The expert systems/local knowledges dichotomy is explicitly linked with themes of colonialism and imperialism. 'Therapy plc' has used a specious version of expert knowledge to colonise and weld into an empire many diverse local craft knowledges – hence distorting them. It has managed to ignore how 'scientific research' itself – the system's own expertise – repeatedly shows that, although therapy seems generally beneficial, *neither technique nor training significantly affect the benefits reported*. What *does* make therapy effective is precisely an ensemble of 'local knowledges' – the 'therapeutic bond' and all the imponderables on which it depends.

Geertz, who coined the term 'local knowledge', also speaks (1973) of 'thick description', an expression borrowed from Gilbert Ryle to indicate the need for *contextuality* in any adequate account of human behaviour. Since context is in principle infinite, Geertz asserts the impossibility of ever *getting to the bottom of things*, quoting the well known story about a Westerner who, told by a native informant that the world rests on a platform which rests on the back of an elephant which rests in turn on the back of a turtle, asks what the turtle rests on? Another turtle. And that turtle? Well, after that it's turtles all the way down.

Domesticated culture, as expressed in phenomena like the state, is constantly trying to shorten the informational food chain, to get to the final turtle. This attempt is distilled in the concept and practice of *expertise*, which is:

> formulated on a global level, that is, within the abstract 'synthetic nature' constructed by science. And the terms it is built on are to be highly standardized, quantifiable and not subject to subjective interpretations. It is through such a model, its language and its terms that the necessary control, manipulation and supervision ... is established.
> (Van der Ploeg, 1993: 219)

Facilitating the client's grounding in their own dense and embodied experience, as a condition of creative change, therapy is a powerful example of both thick description and local knowledge.

Maugrim

In *The Lion, the Witch and the Wardrobe*, the werewolf Maugrim is the White Witch's enforcer, head of the Secret Police. Therapy and counselling have many Maugrims.

Therapy is experiencing a ferocious clash between the 'expert systems' approach and the 'local knowledge' approach: a clash in which expertise always has the debating advantage, because it can speak simply and with one voice – simplification and univocality being two of its essential characteristics. The struggle is not a new one for therapy, which has always held a tension between local knowledge and expertise, thickness and thinness, art and science, wildness and domestication. This tension plays a key role in clinical practice, where training focused on domestication installs a self-censorship or 'therapy police' in practitioners – largely through an unexamined notion of *boundaries* (see Chapter 11, this volume).

This amplifies the self-censorship which already tends to be present. Many supervisors have noticed how their supervisees inhibit their own responses, and in fact their own best judgement, in response to an internal modelling of what they believe is expected of them by their profession. This is natural and to a certain extent appropriate for trainees or newly qualified practitioners, though even here it can be unhelpfully exaggerated; but for experienced therapists it acts as a block to authentic relationship with their clients.

Conclusion

The more complex our society is, the less controllable everything is, so that the striving for control becomes less and less sane, more and more about simplifying not *reality*, but *appearance*. The rise of the 'neo-liberal state' heightens this situation: through an ideological conviction that the free market will magically solve all problems, the state resigns many of its traditional functions, leaving a frightening vacuum (Cooper, 2001). Andrew Cooper highlights the irreality which results from neo-liberal ideology, and the ways in which this relates to deeper psychosocial issues – issues which psychotherapy has traditionally tasked itself with exposing. 'However capable we may be of improving on past performance, in the domain of health, welfare and mental health practice there always will be mistakes, there will be failures and deaths, there will be guilt, anxiety and the wish to blame. These things will not and cannot go away' (Cooper, 2001: 361).

This is not a tame universe, in other words; and therapy has historically tasked itself with saying so, and also saying that this is endurable. But human beings have always found this difficult; and the trend of society at the moment is in the opposite direction, towards the illusion that given enough rules, enough monitoring, enough surveillance, enough punishment, suffering can be prevented. Both individual therapists, and therapy as a profession, will have to choose whether to appease this fantasy, or to stand against it, or to go underground. Lion? What lion?

Part 3
Therapy in the World

13

Upstream Runners and Instream Waders

There is an old Buddhist story (or if there isn't, there should be): two monks are walking beside a fast-flowing river. Suddenly, they hear a shout, and see a man being carried helplessly downstream. Wading into the water, they manage to pull him out, and are tending to him on the bank when they hear a woman's voice and realise that she too is struggling in the torrent. Again, they manage to pull her out; but then they see a whole group of people being swept along. One of the monks is about to wade in for the third time when he realises that his companion is not with him; instead she is running upstream as fast as she can. 'Where are you off to?' he demands. 'These people need help!' Without slowing, the other monk shouts over her shoulder, 'I'm going to find the bastard who's throwing them in!'

This pretty much sums up one central justification for bringing politics together with psychotherapy: that it is not possible properly to understand, or address, individual suffering (people being carried downstream) without looking at the context of power relationships in which it occurs (someone throwing them in). There are some complexities embedded in the story, however. It is fairly clear what the 'upstream runner's' position is: it is less important to relieve immediate drowning than to identify and resolve underlying causative factors leading to drowning. But how would the 'instream wader' respond?

He might argue that what happens upstream is none of his business: he is trained and specialised in rescuing drowning people, not in abstruse analysis of how they got there. (For an explicit statement of this view, see Johnson, 2001a, b.) He might say that, as a compassionate human being, he is compelled to try to save the drowning, whatever the reasons for their being there (and he might prefer to supply lifesaver jackets rather than pull them out of the water). He might take the view that if someone is drowning, it is ultimately for internal rather than external reasons: if someone

---

2006. The opening section of the Introduction to *The Politics of Psychotherapy* (Totton, 2006b), which I edited. It's one of my favourites from my writings.

hadn't thrown them in, they would have jumped in themselves, or found another persecutor to do the job for them – and besides, they could always learn to swim! Another possible argument is that people get in deep waters because they are unwilling to adjust to reality and stay away from the bank.

The 'instream wader' might go further: he might suggest that if someone is indeed throwing people in, then the real question is why. Given time, he might develop a theory (in the moments between rescuing the drowning) that those who throw people into rivers have themselves been thrown in at an early age, and have a compulsion to repeat their own trauma; or alternatively, that the wish to drown others is an inherent aspect of human subjectivity. In fact, some of these ideas might appeal to the 'upstream runner' as well, and she might feel the need to sit on the bank and think about it all for a while. Meanwhile, struggling people are being washed downstream...

The politics of psychotherapy

The point I want to emphasise is that *all* of these positions are *political* – that is, related to issues of power and control in human society (see Totton, 2000: 1–2). If we move from the river to the therapy profession, the view that psychotherapy has no business with the social causes of distress is just as much a political stance as the view that we do indeed need to examine those social causes. In more general terms, it represents a position on citizenship: that the job of the individual citizen is to stick to their last and leave politics to the 'experts', apart perhaps from election time (if the experts let us hold elections). It may well also incorporate an individualist and/or fatalist view of suffering – that people have a hard time because of their personal makeup/human nature/original sin.

All psychotherapists have a political view of their work; because all psychotherapy rests on a theory – explicit or implicit, conscious or unconscious – of *how people should be.* In assessing and working with clients, one is inevitably drawing on a sense of what is a desirable and appropriate state. Is happiness the goal for human beings? Or calm acceptance of the unsatisfactory nature of life? Is happiness attainable through following our own star, or through adapting to the society around us? Should we strive to be useful to others, or concentrate on fulfilling our own potential? One can hardly do psychotherapy without some way of positioning oneself around these and many other questions – even if one's position is that people should be supported in whatever goals they set for themselves. This, just like any other position on these questions about human nature and its needs, is a position not only about individual goals, but also about social and political ones; there is no line to be drawn between the two.

As I argue in Chapters 16 and 18 (and in Totton, 2000), conservative political stances manage a smart piece of camouflage by presenting themselves as *non*-political: since they support the status quo, they can disappear into the default position, so to speak: what is, is natural, because it is. This is no more than sleight of hand, however – in the context of therapy as much as anywhere else. The view that the current situation is one to be approved and encouraged is as political as the opposite view. There have been times in the history of psychotherapy when its job was generally understood as being to support the status quo, and help clients adjust to it (for instance, in the USA in the 1950s); and times when its job was generally understood as being to challenge the status quo and help clients resist it (for instance, in the USA in the 1960s). In both cases therapy was following and legitimising a powerful social trend.

I hope to have established that psychotherapy, far from being politically neutral, is shot through with political judgements. It is also a field of political *action*, a place where power is exercised and contested, as therapists try to affect clients' lives, and clients acquiesce, resist, or do both at the same time. If we add in the 'upstream runner's' view that clients' problems can only be understood within a wider sociopolitical context, then there is surely serious need to explore the politics of psychotherapy – and also, perhaps, reason to be surprised that comparatively little work has been done in this field.

14

Psychotherapy and Politics International: First editorial

There could hardly be a more appropriate time to launch this journal. On the one hand, global politics demonstrates with chilling immediacy the relevance of concepts from across the whole spectrum of therapeutic approaches – denial, dissociation, projection, projective identification, the shadow, scapegoating, dreaming up, and many more. Questions about the nature and origins of human destructiveness, and about what nurtures creativity and peace, have never been more urgent. At the same time, the internal politics of the psychotherapy world are also intense: the impact of political, social and economic factors is generating new regimes of regulation and control, which in turn set off cascading struggles for hegemony between different interest groups of trainers and practitioners. Furthermore, the practice of psychotherapy is encountering profound political challenges: psychotherapists are having to examine their own racism, sexism, and attitude to economic and personal power.

It is also arguable, though, that almost any other time in the last hundred years would have been equally appropriate. Psychotherapy and politics have a long and deep historical relationship (Totton, 2000): from Freud onwards, at least, psychotherapists have both offered to 'put politics on the couch' (Samuels, 2001), and wrestled with political critiques of their own practices and institutions. One interesting question, therefore, would be: Why now? Why has it taken so long for psychotherapy and politics to emerge as an identifiable area of study and interest?

Part of the answer clearly lies in the indefatigable expansion of scholarship into new areas of specialisation, paralleled by the birth of new specialist journals! But we hope that there is more to it than that. The development of psychotherapy and politics as a field of exploration seems to reflect two factors in particular. Firstly, politics itself, in the sense of what politicians do, is increasingly

---

2003. The inaugural edition of the journal which I began with Andrew Samuels, and edited for nine years before handing over to Keith Tudor in 2012.

and unmistakeably bankrupt. More and more people feel a basic contempt for its practitioners, who are visibly confronting events over which they have little control, and about which they have equally little useful to say.

The second, and linked, factor is that psychotherapy emerges more and more clearly as, among other things, the practice of truthfulness. In a world where politicians are seen to lie and lie without remorse or consequence, there is a great need for any source of truth. Psychotherapy is intrinsically concerned with truth and its consequences, untruth and its consequences, and how to distinguish the two. It is by no means the only such practice; but unlike science or philosophy, the truth it studies is not just rational but emotional. And unlike religion, for example, it also tells us, truthfully, that no truth is absolute – that truth is not singular but plural and contingent, and therefore subject to negotiation.

At this point we need to stop, however. The first issue of this journal is not the place to lay down some final editorial position about its subject matter: our intention is rather to use the journal to gather material which helps us to find out about psychotherapy, politics, and their various relationships. The hope is to build up a body of knowledge from which conclusions might eventually be drawn. Thus although there are a number of topics on which we intend to publish papers – for example, political activism by psychotherapists; the psychological roots of racism and sexism; sexuality and gender; therapeutic approaches to conflict resolution; the institutional politics of psychotherapy; ecopsychology; power in the therapeutic relationship – we will be particular excited to receive contributions on subjects about which we have not thought, subjects which we have not yet identified as relevant to our field.

There is at least one way in which PPI itself is taking an active psycho-political position: the journal is not wedded to any single account of the psychotherapeutic process, and will publish material drawn from all schools of psychotherapy. There are startlingly few journals which draw equally from the psychodynamic and humanistic worlds: the split between the two is in some ways equivalent to the Cold War between West and East, and equivalently destructive in its effects. We hope to publish material on this issue.

Similarly, PPI will strive not to limit the political orientation of its contents. We expect this aspiration to cause us pain and hard work: we may well fail to sustain it, since it is easy to imagine submissions we will not want to publish because we disapprove of them politically. This parallels important and difficult questions about clinical practice – what does a psychotherapist do when she deeply disagrees with a client's politics? Ignore them, pathologise them, or argue with them? To the best of our ability, in any event, we welcome controversy to our pages as a vital element in the creative development of our field of study.

15

Psychotherapy and Politics: Is there an alternative?

I have been writing and speaking for some years now on the general subject of psychotherapy and politics (e.g. Totton, 2000, 2005, 2006a, c, d); what follows below is some of my most recent thinking around the issue. Times have changed in the world of psychotherapy from the not very distant days when any political reference was interpreted as a personal one: 'Perhaps the Iraq war reminds you of your family conflicts; perhaps you are sensitive to issues of racism/sexism because you felt that your mother preferred your sister to you ....' Times have changed; but maybe not that much.

Andrew Samuels' groundbreaking book, *The Political Psyche* (Samuels, 1993), demonstrated not only how many practitioners were already quietly working with explicitly political issues, but also just how many therapeutic issues actually have a political dimension. Samuels argued for the importance of addressing both explicit and implicit political dimensions of life. This book inspired and brought together a number of practitioners whose thinking was already heading in similar directions; it also, among other things, helped to inspire the creation of Psychotherapists and Counsellors for Social Responsibility in the UK (http://pcsr-uk.ning.com/), and its sister organisation, Psychotherapists for Social Responsibility, in the USA. A more recent development was the launching nine years ago of the refereed journal *Psychotherapy and Politics International*, from the editorship of which I have recently retired.

So why do I say that times may not have changed that much? Although the acceptance of 'psychotherapy and politics' as a meaningful concept is now much more mainstream than it used to be, that concept still tends to split into two halves, with most people who are interested at all being interested in either one or the other. It seems to be generally agreed that 'political' signifies 'having to do with one kind or another of power'. With not that many exceptions, I find that people are either interested in micropolitics or in macropolitics: either in power relations in the

---

2011. Written by request for the newsletter *Group-Analytic Contexts*.

therapy room and in people's personal lives – politics with a small 'p' – or in what therapy might have to say or to do about large-scale power relations in public political issues, especially conflict of various kinds – Politics with a big 'P'.

I want to try to show in this article that it makes no sense to split micropolitics from macropolitics, and that this is particularly true if one's analysis starts out from a psychotherapeutic worldview. In order to do this I will start out afresh from the basic question – still a live one – of whether therapy and politics belong together at all. Times have changed: the question used to be 'Can therapy be political?' but the new question is 'Can therapy be apolitical?' My answer is that it can't, for two core reasons:

- Even if a person can be an apolitical plumber or an apolitical postal worker, this is not an option for therapists, because we are working with values, and values have an inherent political quality.

- But actually I don't believe one can be an apolitical plumber or postal worker. Just as psychotherapy exposes the unconscious fantasies and emotions within a situation, it also exposes, or can expose, the unconscious politics.

Let me explore each of these points in more detail.

Therapy is inherently political

I have argued this position several times in several contexts, and it still feels important to do so. The nub of the argument is that therapists are always expressing a political position – because their work always and inevitably flows from a view on how human beings should be, and therefore carries a vision of how we could become how we should be (Chapter 16, this volume). However these visions and positions are often implicit rather than explicit, or even held out of consciousness; and this can be problematic – politically problematic, with a small 'p', because this inexplicitness is in effect manipulative of the client.

Taking a view on how human beings should be seems to me intrinsic to our interactions with our clients – however much some therapists would like to believe otherwise. Many forms of therapy aim explicitly at cure and adjustment; with the underlying assumption that we should be healthy and well-adjusted – and of course each therapy and each practitioner has their own definitions of what 'healthy' or 'well-adjusted' looks like. Each believes that their clients should adjust to whatever aspects of life they themselves see as acceptable, as natural; while tacitly assuming that other less acceptable aspects should be resisted (Totton, 2000: 66-8, 106-7). The point, though less obvious, is no less true for more 'permissive' styles of therapy, which take it as their goal to support the client in their authentic, spontaneous growth. Apart from the subtle difficulty of establishing which features of the work represent the client's authenticity, and which their resistance to it, this goal is itself no less a political one than the goal of adjustment: it is founded on a belief that people should be authentic, spontaneous and growthful.

The goals of therapy, then, are always ultimately frameable as social and political goals. The line which many theorists attempt to draw between individual and the social territories is not a real one: what we want for our clients, we necessarily in some sense and to some degree want for society. And as therapists, we are also always needing to navigate within society as it is now constituted: many positions we take within the consulting room are also positions about what goes on outside it.

In therapy, as in the rest of life, claiming to be 'apolitical' generally translates as being conservative (or possibly as being an anarchist). Ultimately, there is no neutrality; what generally passes for 'neutrality' is an active or passive acceptance of the status quo (Chapter 16, this volume). If therapists do not acknowledge (a) that they operate in a social and political context, and (b) that they are agents in that context, then they will be misleading themselves and misleading their clients. This in any case follows from my next point.

Life is inherently political

Whatever the specific fit between psychotherapy and politics, therapy is a human activity; and I believe that every human activity has a political aspect. As Foucault taught us, power twines its way through every relationship and situation; and as Freud and others have also taught us, even the most solitary activities take place in a web of remembered and fantasised relationship. To put it in very simple terms, there are always and everywhere people telling us what to do; and we are constantly implicated in some combination of resistance to, appeasement of, adjustment to, negotiation with, evasion of, collusion with or submission to these instructions.

As a practice which investigates conscious and unconscious motive, psychotherapy is deeply interested in these power relations with both real and imagined others. What we discover is that there is a profound and complex correlation between 'big P' Politics and 'small p' politics. In a sense the traditional interpretations I referred to in my opening paragraph were correct: the Iraq war *does* remind us of our family conflicts, we *are* sensitised to issues of racism/sexism by sibling competition. What was mistaken was the crude reductionism which privileged the personal level over all others. The Iraq war reminds us of family conflicts because the two share similar structures (after all, the war was tied up with an oedipal struggle between the two Bushes). Lines of causality and correlation must always be read in both directions simultaneously: our 'small p' personal histories shape our 'big P' Politics, and what happens in the 'big P' register simultaneously shapes our personal experience. It is never a question of choosing between the two.

It is of course true and important that individuals have different degrees of what Andrew Samuels calls 'political energy' (Samuels, 1993: 57–8, 2001: 16–20). Some people are drawn to issues of power, conflict and social responsibility; others tend to stay in the so-called 'private sphere' and cultivate their gardens. Interestingly, the rise of green politics and the urgency of the ecological crisis mean that cultivating one's garden is no longer a very good image of the apolitical life – gardening has become an arena of political struggle! As the old joke slogan has it, 'Gardeners for a Secure Fuschia'...

Revolutions seem to happen when the implicit micropolitics of everyday life suddenly reveals an explicitly political nature. In ordinary times, only those with high political energy will make the connections. But at certain moments – for example in the Argentinian financial collapse in the early years of this century (Hollander, 2010: Ch 7) – it becomes a self-evident fact that the personal is political and the political is personal; and collective political energy shoots off the scale.

I have experienced similar transformative moments, on a smaller scale, in therapy groups: when individual issues suddenly reveal their collective meaning and vice versa, so that the usual convenient partitions of the world momentarily collapse and we are revealed to be all inhabitants of the same space, who must necessarily negotiate relationships of power with each other. However these moments when a brilliant light falls on everything can be obscured and negated by a facilitator who persistently reduces reality to a family at home. Reminding people of this personal, infantile component of political life can offer a crucial grounding – particularly when it recognises that family life is not an alternative to but a special form of political relationship; but I think there is actually something rather mad, or at least dissociated, about its habitual reductionist use.

This interpretative strategy privileges a couple of specific frames on which the therapist happens to be expert: that of the nuclear family, and that of individual agency. It wrong-foots and disempowers the client or group member, seemingly implying that political engagement itself is intrinsically mad, a misunderstanding of what, in the therapeutic context, matters. An alternative point of view is that such engagement is, as Andrew Samuels has suggested (1993: 57–8, 2001: 16–20), a normal human capacity, a specifically 'political energy' which expresses itself in different styles and with different degrees of strength in each of us.

The politics-avoidant response implies that therapy has nothing to say about politics or society – that therapy is somehow uniquely and wholly apolitical, or even asocial. If this were true, I think it would be a very sad truth; luckily, though, it isn't. Therapy and therapists have a great deal to offer, through practical and theoretical engagement with 'big P' political issues (Totton, 2006b; Chapters 14 and 16, this volume), and – perhaps even more so, since we are uniquely placed to explore this area – through an analysis of the 'small p' micropolitics of personal life.

16

Can Psychotherapy Help Make a Better Future?

I want to argue first of all that the question posed in the title of this conference is misplaced. Rather than 'Is therapy the future?' we should be asking 'How can we, people involved with therapy and counselling, help to make a future?' And this of course depends in turn on what we want that future to be.

I don't believe that therapy is the future. But I do think that therapy can potentially contribute to creating a better future, not just for humanity, but for the whole planetary web on which we depend. However, there are no guarantees of this: therapy also has the potential to make things even worse. It depends entirely on which model of the future prevails within the therapeutic community.

Psychotherapy is famous, of course, not for its vision of the future but for its vision of the past. Its founding claim, in a sense, is that both present and future are conditioned by the past, and that only by understanding this relationship in our own lives can we become free to create a future which does not repeat the past. So straight away we come to a position on the future – one which is actually very close to Marx's view, that only by understanding the past can we escape repeating it.

But I want to explore another way in which therapy always entails a position on the future: because it always has positions on *how human beings should be*, and thus always carries a vision of how we could come to be what we should be. These visions and positions are often unconscious and implicit – and this can be dangerous.

Perhaps I should explain a bit why I say that therapy always has positions on how people should be. It seems to me that this is an inevitable part of our whole approach to interacting with our clients. This is very obvious with therapy approaches that think explicitly in terms of cure and adjustment: people *should be* healthy, *should be* well-adjusted – and of course each school and each practitioner has their own set of small print about what 'healthy' or

---

2004. A lightly edited version of a keynote address to the BACP conference 'Is therapy the future?' which was published in 2005 in *Psychotherapy and Politics International*.

'well-adjusted' actually means. 'Well-adjusted' to what? Each practitioner believes that their clients should adjust to whatever aspects of life they themselves see as natural or acceptable. An entire political programme can be unpacked from the phrase 'well-adjusted'.

As I say, this is more obvious with therapy approaches which explicitly seek cure or adjustment. But it certainly doesn't only apply to such systems. One area where this is particularly apparent is in relation to sexuality: we each have our own ideas about what constitutes normal sexual behaviour, and we inevitably apply these to our work with clients. It is actually not at all easy for us even to make our own ideas about sex available for our conscious minds to think about. We can spend years in therapy achieving this. Consciously or unconsciously, we listen to our clients talk about sex through the filter of our own sense of what is OK or not OK; and consciously or unconsciously, our clients pick up this response in us – pick up our sexual politics. Consciously or unconsciously, we will seek to move our clients towards a view and a practice of sex which is closer to our own. (For a good discussion of many issues around sexuality and therapy, see Denman, 2003.)

One possible position which we may take, of course, is that we accept, or try to accept, any sexual behaviour which makes our clients happy. (We may or may not agree unconsciously with this conscious position.) And that in itself is a political position – a liberal one – that any sexual behaviour is acceptable so long as its participants are happy.

It seems to me that ideas about how people should be are equally present in more process-oriented approaches, which try to avoid prescription and aim to follow and support whatever arises, whether or not this matches the practitioner's goals or expectations (e.g. Mindell & Mindell, 1992). Personally I see this as a splendid intention, and one which I try to apply in my own work; but even if we succeed in this quite difficult project, it is still based on a set of beliefs about how people should be. For a process-oriented practitioner, people *should be* spontaneous, we *should* follow our unconscious wisdom rather than try to control it, things *should be* left to sort themselves out in their own way – again, an entire political programme.

Many people have the habit of drawing an imaginary line between a programme for individuals and a programme for society – as if it was possible to have one without the other. But our position on how individuals should be necessarily entails a position on how society should be organised – whether we like to accept this or not. If individuals should be a particular way, then obviously society should be organised so as to permit and support this way of being; and this may or may not already be the case. If our position about individuals is a conservative one, then our position on society will also be conservative: that everything should stay more or less as it is, or perhaps go back to how it was when we were a bit younger. In that case our programme can stay more or less invisible: everything is all right as it is. But in reality, this is no less a programme than one which wants people and society to change.

Let me emphasise that I am not saying there is anything wrong with this. We're human beings, we have beliefs about how things should be, how people should be. Some of those beliefs, in my view, are more compatible with the working of psychotherapy than others, and I'll say more about that later. But operating from a set of beliefs is in no way wrong, in fact it is inevitable. What I do think is bad practice is to pretend that we are *not* operating from a set of beliefs, or that those beliefs are different from what they really are. Then we confuse both our clients and ourselves.

And these beliefs, as I have said, entail a position on the future: a vision of what sort of world we would like to see emerging. We may or may not be trying to do anything about this; we may or may not think that our practice of psychotherapy is a way of affecting the future. But we do, *as psychotherapists*, have a position about it.

At the moment one can identify two primary positions within therapy which have explicit agendas for the future, both of therapy and of the planet. I'm going to call these positions *therapy as an expert system*, and *therapy as a social critique*. This polarity goes back a very long way – at least to the 1950s, and probably to the origins of psychotherapy more than a century ago (Jacoby, 1977); there have always been practitioners on both sides of the polarity, and no doubt there always will be.

So I'm going to take a little time to explore each side of the polarity. You probably won't find it hard to guess on which side I place myself – but this doesn't mean that I only see merit in my own point of view. One of the things which therapy offers society, as we will see later, is an understanding that in every polarity, there is something of value on both sides. It's actually in some ways very hard to choose between these alternatives; and really we all combine elements of all of them in our work. However, the expert systems approach has had a lot more press in recent years; so some rebalancing is probably in order.

Expert systems/local knowledge

I have described at length in Chapter 1 the distinction between an expert systems model of therapy, and a local knowledge(s) model; and have looked at why the drive to professionalisation of psychotherapy and counselling has entailed a move towards the former and away from the latter. The expert systems approach tends inexorably towards the position that there is a single activity of therapy, with variations which are ultimately insignificant. The local knowledge approach, on the other hand, indicates that there is an inherent pluralism to the activity of therapy (Samuels, 1997/2011): that each practitioner, and indeed each client – or even each session – generates a micro-variety of therapeutic practice which is, hopefully, the form best suited to that particular interaction. Just because hundreds of kinds of therapy all work equivalently well doesn't mean they are all doing the same thing. To draw a dramatic analogy, there are hundreds of ways of having sex, many of which are equally effective; but they are definitely not all the same – and each of us prefers some to others.

What, in any case, does 'effectiveness' mean in this context? What is involved in therapy 'working'? This brings us back to my initial point, that every form of therapy and every practitioner is operating from some set of assumptions about how people should be, from which they derive their understanding of what they are up to as therapists or counsellors. Expert systems therapy tends to operate from a cure or adjustment model; local knowledge therapy tends to work from a model which favours following process, sitting with difficulty, and allowing things to work out.

Now, each of these approaches tends also to imply a particular view of society and its needs – a particular agenda for the future. The expert systems approach aligns therapy with a much wider current social emphasis on expertise and qualifications: what we might call a technocratic attitude to the future, the attitude of New Labour and its equivalents elsewhere which assume that issues which used to be about political *argument* are now a matter of specialist *administration*. Hence statements like this:

> Psychotherapists are uniquely qualified and experienced in the understanding of what people need for a satisfying life. ... We need to establish firm pathways of training and psychotherapy provision so that the emotional needs of European citizens can be attended to.
> (Tantam & van Deurzen, 1998: 133–4)

'What people need for a satisfying life' is here treated as a question of *fact;* a satisfying life is something to be provided *for* us by specially qualified personnel who attend to our every 'emotional need', like air hostesses of the psyche. What is being elided here is that in our society many aspects of life, for most people, provide little opportunity for satisfaction: our social system drains both work and leisure of all meaning and enjoyment. Hence the job of therapists, so long as the system itself cannot be questioned – because therapy is trying to establish itself as a profession within that system – must be to find artificial means of re-injecting some sort of satisfaction into the emptiness; of adjusting the individual to the system.

In effect, then, through the expert systems approach therapy is being integrated into advanced capitalism. The American therapist Maureen O'Hara describes the current American situation in exactly these terms:

> Managed care spokespeople openly describe their revolution as the industrialization of health care and, with unconcealed enthusiasm and frequently contempt, declare that the days of 'therapy as a cottage industry' are over. What is happening to therapists in the 1990s is equated with what happened to butchers, bakers and candlestick-makers in the 1800s.
>
> (O'Hara, 1997: 24)

The local knowledge approach, although as I have said it inevitably does take a position on the future, does not do so explicitly; it tends very much to keep its head down and stick to practice. But for my purpose here, the relevant opponent of expert systems psychotherapy is not so much the local knowledge approach, but an approach which understands therapy as a form of social critique; even more than that, as a component of social resistance, one element in a struggle against precisely the social and cultural trends which expert systems therapy tends to support.

This sort of therapy bears witness to the oppression of body and spirit in advanced capitalist society; and, by supporting the inherent processes of resistance and creative expression within individual clients, necessarily encourages their de-adjustment to the system. When Wilhelm Reich worked as a psychoanalyst in the Vienna free clinic in the 1920s, offering full analytic treatment to ordinary working people, what he noticed was that as his patients' therapy unfolded they became less willing to work in boring and exhausting jobs, less willing to stay in miserable relationships, less willing to obey orders without questioning them (Reich, 1942/1973: 175–7). The central question is: is this a good thing or a bad thing?

My personal answer is no doubt already clear to you. But what is important to me here and now is to argue, as I have done, that this question and other questions about how our society is organised are relevant to the practice of psychotherapy – in fact, that the way each of us works as a therapist entails a particular set of answers to these questions; and that we, and our clients, are better off if we are consciously aware of this.

I am also arguing that it makes a difference what vision of the future we as therapists hold. This vision will communicate itself through our work to our clients, and through our stance as an occupational group to society as a whole. I am not arguing here that therapists have a privileged claim to expertise on how our future should unfold, and what needs to be addressed for that to happen. I'm not talking about *privilege,* but about *responsibility.* Rightly or wrongly, how we see things is taken seriously – more and more so as therapy's social position becomes more solid. I believe that we have a responsibility to reflect on our vision of the future; and to offer our energy towards making that vision into reality.

In a sense, then, everything I have said so far is a preamble – an unavoidable and I hope interesting preamble – to what follows. I want to talk about *how* we can help create a better world: to identify and explore four possible areas of contribution by psychotherapy and counselling to our collective human future. There are many other possibilities, but these four areas are of particular interest to me. They are: our understanding of conflict; our understanding of trauma; the developing field of ecopsychology and ecotherapy; and, most fundamental of all, the use of the therapeutic relationship itself as an arena for exploring issues of power.

Conflict

Therapy has always had a high awareness of conflict, on every level from the internal to the interpersonal, the group, and national or international. We have developed a sophisticated understanding of how conflict works, and how all these different levels interconnect with each other. The core of this understanding, for me, is the simple but powerful concept of projection.

This is a very good example of an idea which is enormously familiar to many therapists and counsellors, but often not understood at all by people outside our occupation. If there is a part of myself which makes me angry or ashamed, a part of myself which I cannot accept as Me, then I will imagine that part to be outside myself: I will perceive and experience it in the Other, and hate and attack it there rather than hating and attacking myself (Klein, 1975; Segal, 1988). This in no way implies that there are no real, objective reasons for conflict between people. We fight oppression, we struggle over scarce resources – these are authentic causes. But projection occludes these root causes from our awareness, makes it very hard to get to them, and very hard to negotiate a way through them. It is our experience of the alien and intolerable Other, it seems, which locks us into irrational conflict: into racism, sexism, religious hatred, xenophobia of all kinds. It also allows us to be manipulated into conflict by those who will benefit from it in terms of profit or of power.

Now, many therapists have already involved themselves in practical projects around conflict all over the world – in Northern Ireland, former Yugoslavia, Palestine, South Africa, and many other places (Audergon, 2005). Usually, they have brought together members of all the identified groups in each place, and set up structures for them to listen to each other.

That seems to be all it takes. If people can stay in the same room long enough to listen to each other, then they start to recognise similarities in their experience. Instead of identifying the Other as alien, they begin to experience the Other as Like Me, as another self, another human being. It's as simple and as complex as that; and of course what is hard is supporting people who have hated each other for centuries to stay in the same room long enough for this process to start working. Actually, often it's even harder to get people to come to the same room in the first place – facilitators are already working with a self-selected group, with the individuals who sense and intuit that something needs to change.

In order to stay in that room, participants need, among other things, to find ways of interrupting the reflex of pride. The biggest motor of conflict between communities seems to be pride and injury to pride: the sense that there are some statements that it actually injures my selfhood to hear, experiences which cannot be tolerated because they involve unbearable 'loss of face'. Diplomats are people who deserve our full respect because they understand this, and have learnt ways to interrupt their own reflexes of pride and shame, and to *keep talking*. Hence the wonderful epigram by Hans Blix, 'The noble art of losing face/Will one day save the human race' (Younge, 2003).

Seeing the Other as another self involves re-owning my projections onto them. In order to do this, I have to have ways of tolerating internal conflict, accepting that I have more than one feeling or belief at the same time, managing the anxiety this brings up – Who am I *really*? – and setting up communication and dialogue within my own psyche in what are essentially the same sorts of ways that I have been talking about setting up dialogue in conflict situations. This process can begin to take us beyond the dualism of black/white, good/bad, self/other, which is the *easiest* way to deal with internal conflict, but a way that creates enormous cascades of social damage.

Hal and Sidra Stone wrote a very good piece about this (Stone & Stone, 1994). It's an open letter to President Bush, in which they very respectfully and gently urge President Bush to do exactly what I've said, to pay attention to all the different voices and positions inside himself and let them enter into dialogue. After this was published, I came across an article in the *New York Review of Books*: apparently one of the President's repeated – and deeply depressing – maxims is 'I won't negotiate with myself' (Powers, 2004: 5).

I don't want to get on George Bush's case here, but there's another story about him which is very relevant. Apparently, when he was a child, his young sister died of leukaemia. His parents never held a funeral. Trauma makes it hard to negotiate – internally or externally. And this is where I want to move next.

Trauma

Over the last few decades, individual trauma has moved steadily from the edge towards the centre of therapeutic awareness. It has shown itself to be a powerful clinical and theoretical tool in understanding the experience of many, many people. There is now widespread agreement that traumatic experiences of violence, abuse or loss in childhood can have a permanent and profound effect on the traumatised individual, structuring their style of responding to new events, creating patterns of dissociation or hyperarousal, both of which involve a disconnection from here-and-now reality; together with a tendency to re-enact traumatic experience, damaging oneself and/or others (Perry et al, 1995; Schore, 2000).

More recently, the question has repeatedly been asked: if so many millions of people worldwide have had their lives structured by trauma – psychologically, neurologically, physiologically – what are the implications for society as a whole? How do traumatised individuals, with their burden of dissociation, hyperarousal and denial, come together into a group, and what distortions affect the functioning of that group (Bloom, 2004a, b)?

However, societal trauma is not just 'individual trauma writ large' – not just the statistical aggregate of repeated instances of sexual and physical abuse, deprivation and loss (Elliot, Bishop & Stokes, 2004: 9). This would be serious enough. But societal trauma also describes structural changes on the macro level which result from events like war (especially civil war), famine, plague, ethnic cleansing: erasures and mutilations in the social contract itself, as the holes in the fabric of civil society are filled with malignant substitutes for real bonds of love, care and responsibility – substitutes which are passed on as an inherited viral load to society's children and become part of permanent social reality.

These traumatic adaptations are not just features of the present or the future: they have *already happened* in our society's past. In parallel ways to traumatised individuals, traumatised societies can perhaps become dissociated or hyperaroused; can lose touch with here-and-now reality; and can re-enact their own trauma in ways which damage themselves and others. Some plausible examples of this sort of re-enactment might be the rise of the Nazi party in Germany as a response to the trauma of World War I; and the oppression of Palestinian Arabs by Israel as a response to the trauma of the Holocaust. We might also want to ask ourselves how the death of a whole generation of young British men in the trenches of World War I, or the experience of the Blitz in World War II, are still working their way through our own society.

Trauma is not only a matter of extreme and dramatic experiences; we all, literally all, suffer the effects of ordinary sub-critical trauma, the experience of being born and growing up in a nuclear family in a patriarchal and capitalist society. What I have just called the 'real bonds of love, care and responsibility' have always existed in struggle and competition with malignant patterns of relationship, which psychotherapists (and others) have often taken to be inbuilt and inevitable aspects of human existence. There is now a growing movement of thought which argues that cruelty and malice are perhaps not part of our instinctual structure, but the effect of societal adaptation to trauma. Perhaps, as some therapists have always argued, human beings are kind and loving at our core, and only become otherwise through deprivation and oppression. Is this naïve optimism? – Or is the opposing 'tough realism' itself in fact a traumatised compensation?

I also want to point out that I have been presenting these issues in a dualistic way, as either/or, black/white alternatives. I have already suggested – and it would need a lot more time to argue this fully – that dualistic thinking is itself a response to trauma and the unbearable internal splitting it causes; the internal split is projected out onto the world.

Ecopsychology

This leads on nicely to the third strand I want to explore: the relatively new movement that goes by the names of 'ecopsychology', 'ecotherapy', and other similar variations. Ecopsychology asks the question: how come we have allowed the world to get into the sort of mess it's in? How can we tolerate, and even largely ignore, the environmental catastrophe which surrounds us, the loss of species, the pollution and contamination of great swathes of the biosphere, the greenhouse effect and all it means for us and the rest of the natural world? How can we all – and I seriously do include myself in this – continue to act in ways which we *know* are damaging to our environment, ourselves, other species, our children and grandchildren – all for the sake of a minor convenience or luxury (Roszak, Gomes & Kanner, 1995)?

Well, immediately the danger arises that you will hear this as a broadcast from your own internal critic, and quite rightly and reasonably switch off. This is one of the fundamental difficulties that ecopsychology faces: we don't want to think or talk about these questions. They make us feel bad.

So let me try posing a different question, or the same question in a different way. How can we more deeply feel and express our love for the living world? Our passionate, heart-opening response to the unbelievable, magical beauty of the plants and animals around us?

It seems to me that if we were in living contact with that response in ourselves, then we would necessarily live differently. Something has damaged and deadened our responsiveness to nature, alienated us from it – in fact the simple use of that word, 'nature', to describe something *other than ourselves*, something *we* are not part of, is incredibly revealing. We are talking about dualism again – that we are living within an apparent opposition between 'human' and 'natural', between 'civilised' and 'wild', which allows us to think of nature as something we have the need and the right to control and use for our own benefit – rather than to experience other species as beings to love, venerate, respect and learn from – beings with whom we ultimately share community.

Ecopsychology has come up with a number of models to explain this alienation; but for me, once again, we are looking at the effects of trauma. Dissociation, splitting, deadening, re-enactment of abuse – we see all of these things happening in our relationship with the biosphere (Glendinning, 1994). We also see a very powerful addictiveness working itself out in our patterns of over-consumption which have led to so much ecological damage, and I think addictiveness is also a response to trauma.

If you accept for a minute my emphasis on patterns of individual and societal trauma as the key to understanding a range of destructive social phenomena, then we need to ask ourselves: what can we as therapists do about this? Obviously we can work with individual trauma, and hope that this will have a knock-on effect. But how can we offer therapy to the whole culture? As Freud pointed out many years ago, we cannot expect society to turn up at our consulting room door (cf. Samuels, 2001).

Well, one thing we can do is to keep talking about these issues, naming the role of societal trauma. Over the last century, many concepts which originated in psychotherapy have worked their way through into general cultural awareness, and this does over time make a difference. Another thing we, or at least those of us who feel drawn to this work, can do is to facilitate groups of various kinds to look at how trauma is affecting our actions and experience. I have already mentioned working in areas of inter-community conflict – also a tremendous amount of good work is going on with survivors of traumatic conflict, trying to ensure that the trauma is not simply knocked on into the next generation to repeat itself in acts of mutual revenge.

But as regards the environmental crisis, of course, we are all in the front line, all in the combat zone. And what ecopsychologists have found is that, in order to start addressing these issues, many people need help in opening up to their despair about the future. In a very real sense, our culture is dancing on the edge of the volcano: it is exactly because we know how grim the future looks that we are unable to look at it, unable to do anything about it. The Buddhist activist Joanna Macy (Macy & Brown, 1998) has developed a very powerful structure called 'despair and empowerment work', which facilitates people in going down into their grief, rage and hopelessness about the future of the planet, and then to turn upwards again with a new sense of power to effect change. This applies not only to ecopsychology, but to any sort of social activism for change. We need to *give up* before we can start to work in a creative way.

Exploring power in the therapeutic relationship

I do want to suggest, though – and this is my fourth and final example – that our work in the consulting room can itself offer a very important contribution to creating a better future. Partly this is because people who are more in touch with their needs and feelings will usually find ways to try to get those needs met, and this will be beneficial for society as a whole. But I want to focus on one specific aspect of therapy work: that it is directly and inevitably about *power*.

In a dyad where each of two people has exactly one vote on what constitutes 'reality' – and can use a wide range of techniques to influence how the other person uses their vote – very early hurts around power, autonomy and validation can be re-experienced and transformed; if mishandled, they can also be reinforced.

The most obvious way, it seems to me, that as therapists we can mishandle the situation, is to claim that because we are therapists we have more than one vote on the reality of the situation. This is a mistake to which the expert systems approach is perhaps rather vulnerable: the claim that my expertise, my specialist knowledge, my insight into the human heart and its foibles, entitles me to an extra vote. Unfortunately, irritatingly, this is no more true of the therapy relationship than it is of a parliamentary election.

I want to offer an account of what happens in a successful therapeutic interaction, using the analogy of what happens when two language groups encounter each other (McWhorter, 2000). If the members of one language group are considerably more powerful than the other group – for example, if they have guns and the others don't – then the second group simply learns the first group's language. But if the two groups are roughly equal in power, or if each wants something the other group can provide, then a new form of communication develops between them: what is known as a *pidgin,* an artificial language using an extremely simple syntax, and vocabulary drawn from the languages of both groups.

A pidgin is not a natural language. To put it simply, you could say that it isn't alive: it won't develop, generate new words and concepts, become a medium for poetry. However, once children are born who grow up speaking it, a pidgin is transformed: it becomes what is called a *creole,* a new natural language as creative and infinite in its potential as any other language on earth.

This, it seems to me, is what needs to happen in therapy. First of all the client and practitioner create a pidgin, put together from elements of the language which each person brings with them. But if there is a fertile exchange between therapist and client, a creative intercourse, then a new language is born, a creole, a vessel for new thoughts and feelings that did not pre-exist in either original tongue.

What much more often happens, I fear, is that the therapist overawes the client – who may well want to be overawed! – into *learning the therapist's language.* And, of course, speaking the therapist's language, the client will only tell us what we know already.

Making the client speak our language is only one of many possible ways in which, as therapists, we can re-enact our clients' early trauma. Most children grow up forced to speak their parents' language, not only literally but symbolically. Most children, I think, have painful experiences of being misunderstood, or worse, not listened to in the first place. In this area in particular, but also in a number of other ways, it is almost certain that at some point we will repeat our clients' early painful experience. This can be minimised, but not avoided. And it is the way in which we negotiate this painful and difficult situation – our ability, if you come right down to it, to identify and acknowledge our mistake and to apologise – which decides whether the therapeutic encounter will be a reinforcement of early experiences of powerlessness, or a site where new experiences of empowerment can take place. This, I suggest, is where we can most directly influence the future, for good or for ill.

Conclusion

The most important thing about therapy, perhaps, is that it is *a practice of truth*. In a world where politicians are seen to lie and lie without remorse or consequence, there is a great need for any source of truth. Psychotherapy is intrinsically concerned with truth and its consequences, untruth and its consequences, and how to distinguish the two. It is by no means the only such practice; but unlike science or philosophy, the truth it studies is not just rational but *emotional*. And unlike religion, for example, it also tells us, truthfully, that no truth is absolute – that truth is not singular but plural and contingent, and therefore subject to negotiation. This is perhaps the greatest realisation of modernity, a profoundly transformative knowledge: there is no absolute truth.

If we look at the state of the world in 2004 – the accelerating rate of climate change, and the complete inability of the global political classes to take it seriously; the general degradation of the environment, the die-off of species, the constant eruption of new damage and threats of damage to the planet; the equally endemic spread of large-scale and small-scale violence around the world; the almost universal oppression of women and children, and the widespread oppression of people of colour; and the continuing omnipresence of poverty and its evil twin, greed – there is much reason to despair about our future. And despair, of course, in a vicious downward spiral, breeds apathy, self-centredness and denial. Despair makes it hard for activists to keep going, and hard for most of us to become activists. Shying away from the pain, we shy away from life.

But despair encountered and endured has a tremendous treasure in it; and therapy knows this, knows that often the only way forward is *through* our pain, rather than around it, and that when we can allow ourselves to directly experience our 'unbearable' feelings, they tend to transform. This knowledge is generally applied only on the personal level, in the consulting room; but it is also a vital political understanding. The willingness to tolerate and sit with despair is one of psychotherapy's contributions to political life.

In this paper I have described some of the different agendas for psychotherapy and counselling which are currently in play; and some of my own beliefs about how therapy can potentially be of use to this battered world we live in. I have sketched out, in effect, one possible future, and indicated why it is my preferred option. But the future of psychotherapy and counselling, just like the future of our society in general, is still in contest.

17

Democracy and Therapy

I expect that some readers will be surprised and puzzled by the combination of these two ideas, democracy and therapy. What do they have to do with each other? Quite a lot, I want to suggest; but to explore how therapy connects to democracy (and vice versa) I first need to look at the concept of democracy itself.

Democracy is quite a hot potato at this point in time. It has become the rallying cry for many different, and often opposing, points of view. All over the world today, there are struggles around the issue of democracy – what it means, how it works, what it's worth. George Bush and Tony Blair want to create democracy throughout the world – by force if necessary. This raises two tricky questions: first of all, can democracy be established at gunpoint, or is this a contradiction in terms? And secondly, is what we have in the UK and the USA really democracy – is it, as Bush and Blair claim, the gold standard by which all other political systems should be measured?

What we have in the UK is *representative democracy*. More technically, it employs 'free representation'; this means that we elect individuals who are then free to do whatever they (or their parties) wish. Our only control over them is the possibility of throwing them out at the next election. Until recently, parties held their election manifesto sacrosanct, since this was the agenda on which we voted; this at least paid lip service to the idea that it is the people who decide. Increasingly, however, New Labour feels free to go against its manifesto and bring in policies different from those it promised.

All of this is obviously a long way from people having control over the fabric of their lives. ('Demo-cracy' means 'people power'.) How much say do any of us have in how our taxes are spent? How our workplace is organised? What happens in our locality? Or when 'our' government goes to war? Certainly we can make our opinions known – this is a very important freedom – but no one is obliged to

---

2007. An article I wrote for *Therapy Today* partly in order to publicise an Independent Practitioners Network conference on this theme.

pay any attention. Increasingly, it seems, a sense of powerlessness and alienation from the political process is turning people away from exercising the rights we do have – even the right to vote.

Our contribution

So, again, what does this have to do with therapy? Well, therapists working with groups have a great deal of experience in attending to all of the viewpoints which are present in the group – even unconsciously held ones – and bringing them into dialogue with each other. In fact, there are many facilitators around the world working in global 'hotspots' on issues of conflict and reconciliation, bringing together members of hostile communities – Palestinians and Israelis, Serbs and Croats, Irish Catholics and Protestants – and finding ways for them to recognise their shared humanity and start to communicate (Audergon, 2005). A set of skills and understandings is being established here which, it seems to me, could be an enormous resource for supporting *direct* democracy, rather than representative democracy – a state of affairs in which no one needs to be represented, because every voice and viewpoint is fully *present*.

This is what the well-known psychotherapist Arnold Mindell calls 'Deep Democracy', which he says rests on 'that special feeling of belief in the inherent importance of all parts of ourselves and all viewpoints in the world around us' (Mindell, 1992: 13). As Mindell emphasises, deep democracy is an ancient and universal concept and experience; it is surely also central to what therapy is all about, both with individuals and with groups. Perhaps, then, we have something to offer the wider world as it struggles to deepen democracy on every level, to move from 'majority rule' – or even 'money/power rule' to control over our own lives. This struggle seems to me even more urgent in the light of the ecological crisis and the threat of climate change: not only do governments need to listen to their peoples, but human beings need to listen to the voices and needs of other species and the whole planetary ecosystem: deep democracy means deep ecology.

Regulation

At the same time, though, issues of democracy hit home within the world of therapy and counselling itself. The government is currently seeking to impose regulation through the Health Professions Council, with little consultation of practitioners themselves; or rather, we are being asked for our views on how the details of the arrangements should be laid out – exactly what 'competences' should be ascribed to therapy and counselling – but not whether this is the right way to proceed with regulation; and certainly not whether state regulation should happen at all. Is this democracy?

The large professional organisations for psychological therapies are starting to protest about the government's plans; but only because these have turned out to be different from their *own* plans for state regulation, which they were equally willing to impose without real consultation. Perhaps these organisations might now want to reconsider on what basis they claim to 'represent' their members. This is particularly glaring in the case of UKCP, which up to now has not even had individual membership at all, while still claiming to somehow 'represent' practitioners. But to what extent do the policy decisions even of BACP actually derive from the views and wishes of its members? There is at least a debate to be had here about how therapy and counselling should organise themselves – and whether we shouldn't do this on the basis of what we know as practitioners about people and groups, rather than leaving many of our skills and understandings at the door of the meeting. Increasingly, we are being 'represented' by people who are not even practitioners themselves.

Power in the therapy room

I may be stepping on some toes already, but I'm afraid I need to go even further – democracy, taken seriously, is a powerful solvent! I want to explore how democratic our practice is. Within the therapy room, who decides what is true and what is false, what is 'real' and what is 'illusion'? Practitioners have a great deal of power to control how things are interpreted, and they very often use it. As Anna Sands points out,

> Psychotherapy is the only profession where the practitioner can be insensitive, evasive, patronising, arrogant, discourteous, self-righteous or just plain wrong, and where clients' observations of this can be taken to be an expression of *their* problems, evidence that what they really need is more of the same therapy.
> (Sands, 2000: 15)

David Mearns and Brian Thorne suggest that, at the start of working together, 'the counsellor holds nearly all the cards in a game of which the client does not even know the rules' (1988: 98). So is genuinely informed consent to psychotherapy possible, when no one can appreciate in advance what it will be like, however much it is explained to them (Hinshelwood, 1997: 101–2)? Even when the client learns the rules, they are not the client's rules, but those of the practitioner, or of the therapy 'game' itself. Practitioners can claim that our expertise, our wisdom, our insight into the human heart, entitles us to an extra vote on what rules should apply; but unfortunately this is no more true in a therapy relationship than it is in a parliamentary election (Totton, 2006a).

Readers may be starting to feel anxious and defensive by this point. I share this feeling. After all, like you, I know that I am a reasonably ethical person, with (conscious) good intentions; yet by its structure, therapy can often feel to clients like a 'no win' situation, where someone else always holds the better cards. Rather than trying in vain to eliminate the power struggle from the therapeutic relationship, my suggestion is that we position it centrally, highlighting the struggle between therapist and client over the definition of reality and making it a core theme of our work. Therapy can then be seen as a shared achievement of real power-sharing.

Inner democracy

A further interface between the political and psychological is the idea of inner democracy. Is our internal landscape ruled by a totalitarian dictatorship? Or are the different, often contradictory elements of our plural personalities given space to express themselves? Many forms of psychological practice pay attention to the different 'parts' of each person's psyche – for example, inner critic, inner child, inner teacher – and to the need for these parts to come together and reconcile their different needs and attitudes. This work of tolerating and negotiating with inner difference both encourages us to take a more tolerant and receptive attitude towards outer difference, and equips us to do so – we are less likely to project unwanted parts of ourselves onto other people whom we then attack.

As we have seen, Arnold Mindell emphasises that deep democracy operates on both external and internal levels, and asserts 'the inherent importance of all parts of ourselves and all viewpoints in the world around us' (Mindell, 1992: 13). In 2004 Hal and Sidra Stone, the founders of the Voice Dialogue method for working with subpersonalities, published an open letter to George W Bush, in which they pleaded with him to consult his inner community in the hope that this might influence his policy on Iraq.

> Our deepest concern ... is not the Saddam Hussein that lives in the world. Our deepest concern is the Saddam Hussein that lives in the hidden recesses of your own heart, of our heart, of everyone's heart. If we don't recognise that this kind of energy lives in each of us, we keep projecting it onto the outer Husseins, and that makes it impossible to deal with the darkness in the world in any way other than war.
>
> (Stone & Stone, 2004: 67)

As they themselves recognise, this is a pretty hopeless appeal. One of the most depressing things I know about George Bush is that according to his ex-Treasury Secretary Paul O'Neill, a favourite maxim of the President's is 'I won't negotiate with myself' (Powers 2004: 5).

Deepening democracy

Negotiating with ourselves, however, is what we all need to do; and what therapy helps us to do. As the Stones make clear, in doing so therapy is furthering democracy in the outer world as well as the inner – because these two are not separate but in constant dynamic interaction through mechanisms of projection, introjection and identification. 'Deep democracy is our sense that the world is here to help us become our entire selves, and that we are here to help the world become whole' (Mindell, 1992: 13).

Few people would deny that the world is currently in crisis. Perhaps the world is always in crisis! In any case, this ongoing crisis calls for a response from us – as citizens, and also as therapists. As therapists we certainly don't have the answers; we don't even have the answers for our clients, which as I have argued is an inherently undemocratic and also unhelpful notion. But we do have some good questions; and some good techniques for enabling everyone and every viewpoint to be heard. In their book *Multitude*, Michael Hardt and Antonio Negri (2006) argue that globalisation, while in some very obvious ways it attacks democratic freedoms, also establishes the conditions for a new and more radical expression of democracy, based on pluralism and self-management.

> Every sign of the corruption of power and every crisis of democratic representation, on all levels of the global hierarchy, is confronted by a democratic will to power. This world of rage and love is the real foundation on which the constituent power of the multitude rests.
>
> (Hardt & Negri, 2006: 353)

Rage and love? That sounds like our territory!

18

In and Out of the Mainstream: Therapy in its social and political context

Throughout this chapter, I am going to be considering the therapeutic relationship in two ways. I will be looking at some aspects of the complex set of interlocking contexts within which therapy (by which I mean both psychotherapy and counselling, throughout) is situated, and which define how it is understood by both practitioner and client. I will also be looking at some of the social and political *wounds* which both client and therapist bring to the situation, and which condition the relationship they form with each other.

I hope to show three things in particular: firstly, that both therapy as a process, and satisfying therapeutic outcome, are tied firmly to the social and political context in which therapy takes place. Secondly, that therapists and counsellors exercise political agency in their work, whether or not they are aware of it. And thirdly, that conscious or unconscious support from the therapist for mainstream cultural positions at the expense of the positions of the client can be both wounding and damaging. An unconscious assumption that mainstream views are 'natural' makes it all too easy not only to pathologise wounds – which is a danger for all therapists – but to pathologise difference itself. I have listed these three themes sequentially; but in what follows, they will be found to be firmly braided together, a braid which runs through everything I have to say.

Political dissociation

Like all human activity, therapy takes place in a cultural space which gives it the meaning it has (Erving Goffman's work is helpful here: Goffman, 1997). This is after all very odd behaviour: two people sitting in a room together, while one of them does most of the talking, in often quite unusual styles, about whatever comes to mind, and the other person responds in *extremely* unusual ways which don't always have any obvious bearing on what has been

---

2008. Written for the anthology *The Therapeutic Relationship: Perspectives and Themes* (Haugh & Paul, 2008).

said by the first person. It is validated by a social context which says that it is called psychotherapy or counselling, that it has certain appropriate functions and significances, and that it is socially acceptable and useful. There are also other, simultaneously present, contexts which operate to put the activity of therapy in question, to contest the ways in which it becomes privileged. Some of these contexts are explicitly political, and may suggest, for instance, that therapy can be understood as oppressive and reactionary (Guattari, 1984; Hillman & Ventura, 1993; Masson, 1990), or alternatively as progressive and liberatory (Reich, 1942/1983; Rogers, 1978). For both these contexts, see also Totton, 2000.

Interestingly, though, the discourse of therapy itself often tends to ignore all of these contexts, and to speak as if therapy happens in a social and political vacuum (Samuels, 2006). If the client brings material from the wider social and political situations within which the work is happening, the therapist may very often speak in such a way as to strip the material of this context, to reinterpret it as purely personal and autobiographical in meaning. For example, if the client speaks of their opposition to the Iraq invasion, the therapist may respond by speaking of the client's childhood experience of violence, or their need to oppose authority. The client talks about the government, and the therapist replies about their mother. The client talks about the scars of their working class upbringing, and the therapist replies – as someone reported to me recently – 'When are you going to stop letting that define you?'

Although this kind of response can on occasion be bracing or even liberating, I suggest that there is actually something rather mad, or at least dissociated, about its habitual use. It privileges one or two very specific frames (on which the therapist happens to be expert): that of the nuclear family, and that of individual agency. Like several other common therapeutic strategies (Totton, 2006a), it wrong-foots and disempowers the client, seemingly implying that political engagement itself is intrinsically mad, a misunderstanding of what, in the therapeutic context, matters. An alternative point of view is that such engagement is a normal human capacity, a specifically 'political energy' (Samuels, 1993: 57–8, 2001: 16–20) which expresses itself in different styles and with different degrees of strength in each of us. At the very least, the politics-avoidant response implies that therapy has nothing to say about politics or society – that therapy is somehow uniquely and wholly apolitical, or even asocial.

I believe that this is far from the truth. As we have already seen, therapy always operates within a political and social context, or set of contexts, which give it meaning as a human activity.

More than that, therapy in fact always expresses a political position – because it always and inevitably has a view on *how human beings should be*, and therefore carries a vision of how we could become how we should be (see Chapter 16, this volume). However, these visions and positions are often unconscious and implicit; and I will argue that this can be dangerous.

Taking a view on how people should be seems to me an intrinsic part of our interaction with our clients. There are many forms of therapy which aim explicitly at cure and adjustment; the underlying assumption being that people *should* be healthy and well-adjusted – and of course each therapy and each practitioner has their own definitions of what 'healthy' or 'well-adjusted' looks like. Each believes that their clients should adjust to whatever aspects of life they themselves see as acceptable, as natural, while tacitly assuming that other less acceptable aspects should be resisted. The point, though less obvious, is no less true for more 'permissive' styles of therapy, which take it as their goal to support the client in their authentic, spontaneous growth. Apart from the subtle difficulty of establishing which features of the work represent the client's authenticity, and which their resistance to it, this goal is itself no less a political one than the goal of adjustment: it is founded on a belief that people *should* be authentic, spontaneous and growthful.

The goals of therapy, then, are always ultimately frameable as social and political goals. The line which many theorists attempt to draw between individual and the social territories is not a real one: what we want for our clients, we necessarily in some sense want for society. And also, as therapists, we are always needing to navigate within society as it is now constituted: many positions we take within the consulting room are also positions about what goes on outside it.

As an extreme example of the impossibility of 'apolitical' therapy, take the situation which Juan Pablo Jimenez describes in Chile under Pinochet. The opposition would frequently call for general strikes or stoppages in protest against the regime; almost all organisations, including the medical association, would agree to join in.

> On such days there is no public transport, colleges and universities close their doors and many doctors do not work. Some patients announce that they will not come for treatment. Others distinguish social protests from the act of being psychoanalysed.
>
> The analyst, for his [sic] part, may decide not to work and thus show his patients a political position, or to work, which

> some patients will construe as clear evidence of sympathy with the government. He may decide to work with some and not with others, thus introducing a degree of splitting into his daily work. In any case, on some of these days, at certain times, it may actually be dangerous to pass through certain parts of the city. Inevitably, any decision taken by the analyst will, depending on the patient, have repercussions on the transference and may need to be analysed with the patient. However, this is also not easy. At the time of the socialist government, I knew of a training analysis that was broken off because the analyst and the candidate got into a violent political argument.
>
> (Jimenez, 1989: 501)

This is an extreme example of a situation in which *any* move or non-move on the part of the therapist will be interpreted as – and therefore become – an explicit political stance. But aren't we all in this situation all the time? If the client mentions a current political issue, we have several choices: for example, we can ignore them; we can comment from our own perspective; we can say something like 'You obviously feel strongly about that'; we can make an interpretation in terms of what we know of their personal history; we can employ the all-purpose therapeutic 'Mmm-hmmm'; or we can produce some combination of these responses. However, *none* of these are neutral: they all convey some degree or other of more-or-less nuanced approval or disapproval, certainly of the client's introduction of this theme, but surely therefore by implication of the theme itself and the client's relationship to it.

I would go further. If a client arrives on the day of the Iraq invasion, for example, without any major personal issue to discuss, and yet *does not mention the invasion*, then I suggest that it would be in line with usual therapeutic behaviour to point out this omission, and to ask about it. Is the client so politically autistic as to have not noticed the event? Do they perhaps feel that we would not approve of their mentioning it? Or are they trying to avoid what they see as a potential row with us over our differing views? All of these possibilities are therapeutically interesting, to say the least. If we do not feel that to mention the omission would be appropriate, then what is it about political territory that seals it off so definitively from the therapeutic?

There are many issues and problems clients bring which, it can be argued, are insoluble and indeed incomprehensible without a social frame of reference. The working class client's sense of shame and inadequacy; the female client's anxieties around weight and appearance; the black, or gay or lesbian client's experience of exclusion; the poor client's envy and alienation – does it really make sense to address these feelings therapeutically without considering the social factors which help to create and maintain them? (For therapeutic discussion of each of these, in the same order, see Kearney, 1996; Orbach 1998; Layo & Haugh, 2006; Davies & Charles, 1996.) Lynne Layton has written of what she calls the 'normative unconscious': the ensemble of mainstream understandings of how people should be which very often remain below the surface of awareness (Layton, 2004, 2006; for different approaches to this issue see Kearney, 1996 and Mindell, 1995). If, for instance, we support the female client just mentioned in her sense that she should work hard to be slim and attractive to men, then we may be failing to question our own normative unconscious beliefs, and how they collude with the client's beliefs.

This sort of example raises difficult questions about power in the therapeutic relationship, and the dangers of imposing our own views on the client. However, this danger is hardwired into the therapy situation. Ultimately, there is no neutrality; what generally passes for 'neutrality' is a conservative acceptance of the status quo (Chapter 16, this volume; Totton, 2006a). If therapists do not acknowledge (a) that they operate in a social and political context, and (b) that they are *agents* in that context, then they will be misleading themselves and misleading their clients.

Difference, power and rank

Again like all human activity, therapy occurs within a framework of sameness and difference. The two participants, each being human, are attuned to many dimensions in which they can perceive each other as *similar*, and many others in which they can perceive *differences* between self and other. Both of these perceptions – 'they are different from me' and 'they are similar to me' – can be helpful to or destructive of the therapeutic relationship in quite complex ways. For example, if held by the therapist, 'they are similar to me' can generate an empathic, supportive response; it can also lead to collusive attitudes, or to illusory assumptions that the client means and feels the same things that the therapist believes *he or she* would mean and feel in the same situation. 'They are different from me' can stimulate curiosity and open-mindedness; it can also produce incomprehension and hostility.

Experiences of difference in social interaction are a potent source of the emotional wounds which people bring to therapy. They can also easily be re-enacted and reinforced in the therapeutic relationship. Information is technically defined as 'difference which make a difference' (Bateson, 1973: 428*ff*). I want to look at some of the sorts of difference that make a difference to relationships between people, and to consider what sorts of information we take from them. Much of this information is about comparative rank.

Arnold Mindell, one of the few leading psychotherapists currently addressing social and political issues in their work, describes rank as 'the sum of a person's privileges' (Mindell, 1995: 28). 'Whether you earned or inherited your rank, it organises much of your communication behavior' (ibid: 42). In this society, very few differences are neutral with respect to power and rank. Gender, sexuality, class, ethnicity, income, age, disability – all these carry with them enormous implications for perceived and experienced rank and for actual power (power very often comes with rank, but not always; think of the Queen, for example). These issues have traditionally been referred to in terms of 'majority' and 'minority' groups; however, the disempowered group is not always a minority, either in a specific context or in the world as a whole – for example, there are more females than males in the world, but males are a universally empowered group. Therefore I prefer to use Mindell's terms (1995: 30) and speak of 'mainstream' and 'non-mainstream' groups.

A key feature of mainstream culture and values is that they tend to be invisible to their holders (Mindell, 1995: 37). For someone who identifies with the mainstream, their values are simply how things *are* – reflected back to them constantly from the media, and from every authoritative pronouncement. Well known examples of this include the assumption that everyone is male, white and heterosexual unless specified otherwise; the assumption that representative democracy combined with advanced capitalism is the preferred system for everyone in the world; and the assumption that being 'reasonable' is always a good thing.

Rank is both *perceived* and *experienced*; and how we experience our own rank may not be the same as how another person perceives it. This is particularly true with regard to 'mainstream' rank – the sort of automatic bonus of power and authority which goes with being white, male, middle class, etc. A white, male, middle-class therapist may quite sincerely assert that he claims no superiority of rank over a female working-class person of colour who is his client. But if he is unable to recognise the social *reality* that he has far higher rank than her, and to attend to the ways in which this affects her perception of him and vice versa, then the therapeutic relationship will be damaged from the start. 'Rank is a drug. The more you have, the less aware you are of how it affects others negatively' (Mindell, 1995: 49).

In other words, rank is subject to the phenomenon of the invisible mainstream. In the above summary I may well have left out one or more dimensions of difference which, for you the reader, are deeply significant in terms of rank. If so, this is probably a dimension to which, at this particular moment, I am pretty much blind, and I apologise for this. Similar blindnesses occur in the therapy room; and it is enormously important that therapists are open to being educated by their clients in dimensions of rank of which they have not previously been conscious – and to apologising for the hurt which their unconsciousness creates.

It is also important to realise that some therapists are themselves carrying wounds relating to rank, which may negatively affect their work with certain clients: black therapist with white client, working-class therapist with middle-class client, female therapist with male client – all need extra awareness and work on themselves in order to refrain from persecuting their 'higher rank' clients. Most often, however, the therapist's challenge is to be aware of their own higher rank. Besides the acquired or inherited rank which the therapist brings to their occupation, there is also the rank that attaches to the role of therapist itself.

Psychotherapists and, to a somewhat lesser extent, counsellors, are generally perceived as skilled professionals, with some of the same authority as doctors or lawyers. They are also widely credited with a specific, uncanny and somewhat frightening ability to 'see right through' people and straight to their deepest secrets. Besides these perceptions, therapy is undoubtedly a middle-class occupation, whatever the self-perception of individual practitioners, and therapists are in fact very often white and middle class. The steadily increasing length and cost of therapy training is likely to increase the distance between the median rank of therapists and of their clients.

This distance of rank in itself translates into various sorts of social power – most fundamentally, *the power to define the situation*, to say whose perception is accurate and whose is distorted, who is 'sick' and who is 'well'. The different contexts in which practitioners work will have a large effect on this: someone working in a GP practice will commonly and naturally be perceived as a member of the medical profession whose statements represent some sort of objective medical authority, and this is even more likely to be the case when the practitioner works in a mental hospital.

Expectations and misunderstandings

Differences of setting, cultural background, and rank-related dimensions such as gender, ethnicity, class, sexuality, age, etc will all tend to set up different expectations of the therapist on the part of the client. Most obviously, someone who identifies with a group which is relatively disadvantaged compared with their perception of their therapist will approach the therapist with some blend of wariness, deference, hostility and appeasement. Of course, we all approach our therapists with some blend of these qualities! – but this aspect of the relationship will be amplified by differences of rank, as it will be by more 'authoritative' settings, institutional or opulent, as the case may be.

Similarly, therapists will have different expectations of the client, depending on differences of setting, of rank-related dimensions, and also differences of *therapeutic culture*. By this I mean the particular network of therapy or counselling which the practitioner is plugged into – largely through their training, but also through choices and connections which they may have made since they trained. As a simple example, many therapists expect their clients to sit down and to talk! This may not be immediately apparent to clients whose cultures (based on family, class, ethnicity or whatever) have different expectations; but the client who, for example, strides around the room 'shouting' – that is, speaking in a louder register than the therapist is accustomed to – may well get a negative reaction.

As Mindell has pointed out (1995: 202ff), the communication style of the mainstream (white, Western, middle class) culture can be characterised as *cool* and *linear*. That is, mainstream individuals tend to speak one at a time, and stick to the subject; they may get angry, but they generally keep this within bounds, and strive for reason and articulacy. Some non-mainstream cultures, however, tend to use hot and *non-linear* communication styles, where emotions bubble up freely and the conversation circles around rather than following a straight line.

Neither of these styles is 'right' or 'wrong', 'better' or 'worse' than the other; each has strengths and weaknesses, each is more useful at certain times. But the great majority of therapists are trained and expert in the cool, linear style, and perhaps puzzled and deskilled – and therefore defensive – when faced with hotter and less linear ways of talking. A minority of therapists, conversely, have been trained in 'growth movement' approaches which equally privilege a 'hot', emotive, 'right brain' style; and they will tend to characterise cool communication as 'being stuck in your head'.

The ideal, then, would be for a practitioner to have a range which allows them to accept, respond to and join in whatever communication style the client offers – and in due course, perhaps, to introduce the possibility of using other styles for particular purposes. But even when one is aware of the issues and consciously open to other styles, one can easily be misled by one's expectations. I had a client who was white, but brought up in the Caribbean, and partially identified as black; his accent was a startling jumble, and his communication style was non-linear to the extent that I didn't receive this information about his background for several sessions, and was tentatively considering him rather disturbed! Once he told me about his history, many things fell into place: 'seeing' him as Afro-Caribbean, I could 'hear' him in a way that made sense to me. But should I have needed that information in order to accept him on his own terms? Many families, or even individuals, have idiosyncratic styles and cultures which work for them.

Probably most practitioners would agree that it is the 'naïve clients', those without previous knowledge of therapy or counselling, with whom clashes of expectation can become most challenging. The BBC comedy series about therapy, *Help*, portrays this very well: one new client starts to sit in the chair of the therapist, who gently intervenes, 'That's my chair'. 'But aren't they all your chairs?' asks the puzzled client. And of course there are many symbolic ways in which a client can try to 'sit in the therapist's chair' before they have learnt the unspoken etiquette of the relationship. But perhaps something creative has been lost once the client is house-trained to 'do therapy' properly – that is, in the style to which the therapist has become accustomed. Remember, we do not have to spell out our expectations in order to let our clients know how they should behave. In the heightened atmosphere of the therapy room, the least shift of intonation, the smallest pause or silence, every choice of which statements or actions of the client to respond to and which ones to let pass, all very effectively convey our preferences – even when we do not intend it. The same is true for our values and beliefs (Totton, 2006a: 89ff).

Society's expectations

The public identity of psychotherapy is complex and ambivalent, reflecting some of the deep contradictions in society itself. Yet therapy is alertly responsive to the demands society makes on it; sometimes mediated through the employment market, sometimes expressed in the media, sometimes discerned in the agendas of our clients; so that it tends to absorb these contradictions into its own self-understanding (Totton, 2006c).

One place where we can see this happening is around the idea of 'cure': something which therapy cannot provide, but which most clients are nevertheless seeking, either openly or covertly. And society as a whole tends to look to psychotherapy for 'cures' to problems which it is unable or unwilling to resolve – for example, child sexual abuse, or antisocial behaviour: in both cases, the authoritarian response is punishment, the liberal response, to call on therapists or counsellors for help. Neither group is prepared to look at the deep cultural, economic and political issues involved. Just as individual clients often hope to be cured without having to change, so we are asked to cure deep social problems without addressing their causes.

While therapy is often expected to perform individual and social miracles, it is also feared and distrusted, for several reasons: its zeroing in on what is concealed; its insistence that the causes of human behaviour are complex rather than simple; its mainly positive attitude towards emotions and desires; and its emphasis (still popularly believed in, though not always any longer present) on sexuality. We get called 'shrinks', 'the-rapist', and 'trick-cyclists', and teased about how much money we make from other people's misery. Going to a therapist is widely seen as a combination of major surgery and visiting a prostitute: it may sometimes be unavoidable, but should be done as fast as possible, and certainly without becoming *dependent*. The deep suspicion of therapists' power to do harm emerges most clearly in the repeated moral panics (Pearson, 1983) about psychotherapists as abusers, whether by general incompetence, by creating False Memory Syndrome, or by having sex with their clients.

The issue of dependency has become a major theme of clients in the past few years (Chapter 7, this volume). At initial meetings, people show an increased reluctance to commit themselves to ongoing weekly psychotherapy – a reluctance which is often based on a fear of becoming dependent. Their hope, it seems, is to have as little therapy as possible, for as short a time as possible, so that they can escape before dependency arises. Depending on a therapist is assumed to be a bad thing, a self-evidently good reason for avoiding long-term therapy. Very often, they mention how friends and family talked of the dangers of depending on a therapist.

The largest context for these attitudes is the ever-increasing value which our society puts on independence, autonomy, self-sufficiency (for the next 20 years the number of households in Britain is expected to rise by around 200,000 a year, of which 150,000 will be due to an increase in single people living alone: Seager, 2006). What is striking, though, is how many therapists have adopted anti-dependency beliefs – despite the traditional, and I believe well-founded, therapeutic view that depending on others is not only intrinsic to human existence, but also a valuable and satisfying aspect of it, and that one of therapy's important functions is to offer an experience of safe dependency. Some anti-dependency therapists are led to this view by a critique of power imbalances in the therapeutic relationship (e.g. Bates & House, 2003). A much larger number are practitioners of brief and solution-focused therapies; here the arguments about benefit are inextricable from practical issues, financial constraints and pressures which militate against long-term intensive therapy. If you are only offering six or twelve sessions, dependency is indeed an undesirable development; and a skilled therapist will manage the work so as to avoid it – sometimes in opposition to the client's process.

Power and economics

Some of the arguments around dependency seem to me to be justifications of the unavoidable. Public and private providers – National Health Service (NHS), managed care, the voluntary sector – all find the expense and long timescale of 'traditional' therapies unacceptable; partly because, in our 'independent' culture, people are unwilling to pay higher taxes to fund such processes. So by a shadowy and overdetermined set of negotiations, a virtue is made of necessity.

This is just one example of the pervasive influence of economics on the practice of therapy. Often, ideology is refracted *through* economics: ideological constraints get translated into economic ones, and are then recreated as a theory of good practice. Besides short-term therapy, several other features of public and voluntary provision fall into this category. For example, clients using these avenues to therapy seldom or never have any choice about which form of therapy they receive, or which individual they see. The reasons for this are basically practical – to allow efficient management of time and resources – but they are accompanied by a theoretical picture that makes different practitioners and different therapies more or less interchangeable.

This is just part of a much wider move towards an expertise-based, 'outcome-focused' version of therapy, which I have argued elsewhere is a distorted and reductionist one (e.g. Chapter 16, this volume). We are in a cleft stick here: the expense of private therapy means that, in David Pilgrim's words, 'personal growth is reserved for the rich' (Pilgrim, 1992: 233) – yet when therapy is offered within the NHS and by voluntary sector organisations, while on the one hand it becomes available to many more people, on the other hand it is shorn of many of its most valuable features, indeed in some ways turned into a different activity altogether. (Paradoxically, some of the most complex clients are seen by some of the least experienced practitioners – volunteer trainees.) Obviously enough, the NHS and charitable funders require evidence of 'effectiveness'. Yet to define effectiveness for therapy in the same way that we define it for medicine is to undermine the activity of therapy entirely. And therapists who are trained in this approach will create a wholly different relationship with their clients – who, if they cannot afford private therapy, may in any case be more deferential and authority-accepting.

Conclusion

A great deal more could be said about therapy in its social and political context, and how these impact the therapeutic relationship. I have tried to indicate what seem to me to be the central issues, without over-egging the pudding. The crucial issue for me is to demonstrate that there *are* such contexts, and that they *do* impact the relationship. To assume otherwise, it seems to me, is among other things, to infantilise the therapeutic relationship, treating it as something that happens without reference to the rest of the world. This, of course, is not actually true even of the mother-infant dyad, which is very much affected by the set of understandings about childrearing within which it exists. But there has been a very strong tendency in therapy to 'privatise' both the therapy pair, and the childrearing pair, the latter so often used as a governing metaphor for therapy.

Two individuals who meet for therapy bring with them complex histories as social and political beings. They will recognise and misrecognise each other in ways which are, among many other things, socially and politically inflected. And they will carry traces of social and political projects of many kinds. The attempt to exclude all of this material from the relationship is both hopeless and pointless.

In the 1960s, two psychoanalysts who tried to analyse a young woman member of the West African Dogon tribe, in order to investigate differences or similarities in psychic structure from Westerners, came up against a tricky obstacle. 'It was practically impossible to speak to her alone. A whole group of women continuously took part in everything that occurred within the analytic situation' (Morgenthaler & Parin, 1964: 446). However,

Contrary to what might have been expected, the supervisory group exercised no sort of prohibitive function. Rather, it encouraged the young woman and even the analyst to make their relationship to each other more intense and more intimate. It was not long before they revealed the content of her wishes by making open demands, in words and gestures, for a sexual relationship.

(Morgenthaler & Parin, 1061: 447)

In our individualistic culture, this is not a problem we frequently encounter – or not in such a concrete form. However, does any interaction truly take place 'alone', and outside the supportive or obstructive influences of the larger social group? Although the literal absence of the social group is a fundamental condition of therapy, its symbolic presence and profound effect is an equally fundamental fact. We need to recognise and explore its implications.

19

May '68

This year is the fortieth anniversary of that baseline year for radical politics, 1968. Partly because the '68 generation' has reached a certain age, and attained positions of influence, the anniversary is being very thoroughly treated in the media; the classic black and white photos, exhilarating and agonising by turn, are being reproduced and retransmitted like viral memes of revolution. But are there any hosts available for infection, or are these dead memes being used for purposes of immunisation?

One of the striking things about looking back on the 60s and 70s is the realisation that so many of our beliefs at the time turned out to have been false then, but to be coming true now. The extent and effectiveness of surveillance was much exaggerated in 1968, but hardly could be exaggerated in 2008. The American Empire was a myth in 1968, but not far from (shambolic though still deadly) reality in 2008. Kidnapping and torture by US agencies was actual but underground in 1968; in 2008 it is official policy. And, of course, in 1968 news of environmental disaster was, though present, comparatively marginal by the standards of 2008.

In a strange irony, then, our complaints were accurately prophetic, but our aspirations currently seem far off beam. All of the lifestyle goals, the ones which make no real difference to capitalism, have been achieved – no one cares any longer how we wear our hair – but all of the meaningful goals relating to power and social justice have been abandoned or twisted out of shape. The French have a word for it: *récupération*, a sea change through which what was once serious emerges as trivial, what was confrontational becomes decorative, and Che Guevara is a fashion label.

It is often forgotten or not understood what an important role therapy and counselling played in the radical movements of the 60s and 70s. Reich, of course, was a sort of guiding genius, but much more for his views on sexuality than for his therapy as such.

2008, 2010. A merger of two editorials in issues of *Psychotherapy and Politics International*.

However, there was a powerful synergistic relationship between radical therapy and radical politics, with each inspiring, informing and deepening the other. In the USA, groups like the Berkeley Radical Psychiatry Center and the Chicago-based Changes group looked for ways to work directly in and with oppressed communities, and to make connections between individual experience and social relations which would radicalise and empower their clients (Totton, 2000: 25-9, 68-9).

In the UK, the main emphasis was on the Radical Psychiatry movement and the work of RD Laing and David Cooper; and in both countries (there is no space here to consider the rest of the world, but see Totton, 2000) there were several initiatives to support and maintain the political energy of activists through self-help therapy (Ernst & Goodison, 1981). Erwin and Miriam Polster gave a very clear account of psychotherapy as a liberated zone and a seed bed of social change: 'we live a two-world existence, straddling the atmosphere of the encounter group and the world in which we live our everyday lives' (Polster & Polster, 1974: 25).

Many key humanistic figures – with an element of bandwagon-jumping – produced writings during this period which strongly echoed and supported the radical movements in society. Carl Rogers published *Carl Rogers on Personal Power: Inner Strength and Its Revolutionary Impact* (1978), arguing that the core conditions of person-centred counselling were intrinsically 'a challenging political statement' (1978: 9). The Polsters (1974) took a similar position about Gestalt, relating it to the 'loosening up of poisonous taboos' in society; and of course Perls, Hefferline and Goodman (1951/1973, e.g. pp. 400-1) had already made powerful statements of opposition to conventional values in the 1950s. As for Transactional Analysis, Carl Steiner, a leading figure in its development, was also central in the Berkeley scene and in the journal *Issues in Radical Therapy* (Wyckoff, 1976), and later published the classic *The Other Side of Power* (Steiner, 1981).

With the ebbing of the radical tide in the 1980s and subsequently, humanistic therapy entered the conventional mainstream, at least relative to its earlier positions. Like ex-radicals in every walk of life, veteran therapists tend either to dislike being reminded of their earlier beliefs, or to treat them as relics of a colourful youth. There are, of course, many honourable exceptions: Carl Steiner, for example, continues to fight his corner; Andrew Samuels is an example close to home; and there is a younger generation of Rogerians, in particular, who have taken up the political implications of humanistic therapy (Proctor, Cooper, Sanders & Malcolm, 2006). Anyone who wants to find out the current state of politicised therapy only needs to read the back issues of this journal (*Psychotherapy and Politics International*).

Looking back, it seems to me that the failure of the countercultural movement was a failure to genuinely bring psychotherapy and politics together – to create a revolutionary way of living, feeling, being, which did not simply paper over neurosis (or in some cases psychosis). Much of the anniversary coverage, from both left and right, seems to focus on the criticism that 1968's revolutionary movements were unprofessional, which is, of course, entirely true – few activists had any real idea of what a successful revolution entailed – but is also their saving grace. Professional revolutions turn into historic disasters: people who study how to seize power are people who want to hold onto it. The only revolution worth having is the unprofessional kind, but so far, unfortunately, to little avail. If an unprofessional revolution ever does succeed, it will be because it is conducted by sane human beings; and where are they to arise from if not psychotherapy?

* * *

Victor Jeleniewski Seidler's paper (Seidler, 2010) on remembering 1968 has many resonances for me, and probably for a whole generation of psychotherapists. Seidler rightly speaks of a necessary work of mourning for those of us who shared the enormous aspirations of that period, and the enormous disappointments which have followed. Without wanting to sound too romantic, the generation of 1968 lost a war. But although there were some deaths and wounds, few of them were direct and obvious; the war itself was mostly indirect and invisible to many, the defeat slow and imperceptible. All of which has made it hard to mourn, to recognise our status as traumatised survivors.

It would be absurd to claim that the fate of the losers of the 60s' culture wars is to any degree as grim as that of the losers in most shooting wars. But so far, all the exaggeration has been in the other direction: a pretence that it was all for the best, that Thatcher and Reagan brought the West to its senses, that really we just 'grew up'. And, of course, it is in many ways about 'growing up'; but one important aspect of the 60s, in the field of therapy as elsewhere, was to put into question the automatic privileging of the grown-up over the child, the assumption that young people's idealism and demands for justice are something they can and should grow out of. From the viewpoint of the 60s, all the ex-hippies who are now pillars of the establishment are just so many political prisoners.

Of course the 60s and 70s were full of contradictions, riddled with sexism and patriarchy while preaching 'liberation'. We were naïve and ignorant in many, many ways. But we tried; and Seidler's paper usefully reminds us of many of the good things that have come out of our trying. Among these is the transformation of psychotherapy which took place during this period, and without which this journal would surely not exist. Although much of the radicalisation of therapy has since been rolled back, much of it still stands. And as the wider social struggle was gradually crushed, therapy and counselling became a place of refuge for many survivors, a cultural space where it was still possible to maintain some of those values – in particular, that 'the personal is political'.

20

Editing *The Politics of Psychotherapy*

> The ontological structure of the human being imposes insurmountable constraints upon any form of social organization and any political project.
> (Castoriadis, 1999: 409)

I used the above quotation from Cornelius Castoriadis as the epigraph for my Introduction to *The Politics of Psychotherapy* (Totton, 2006d), because it gives a very challengingly negative answer to a question which I wanted the book to address. Put in very simple terms, the question is: What can psychotherapy tell us about those 'constraints' which our structure as human beings places upon our actions? And what, if anything, can psychotherapy *do* about them?

That our social organisation and political projects are indeed constrained by what is usually known as 'human nature' is one of the key lessons of the twentieth century. Human beings could scarcely have tried harder or more inventively to create the good society; and we could hardly have failed more comprehensively or more agonisingly. But is it really 'the ontological structure of the human being' which wrecks all political dreams; or is it something more contingent, more open to change? And if it is in fact hardwired into our structure, where does this leave us – in despair, or in some version of the depressive position, realistically exploring the scope for limited improvement?

These questions have, I think, been at the back of most Western political thinking since at least the 1980s, when the final hurrah of millennial idealism (if it was indeed final) crashed and burnt under the aegis of Reagan and Thatcher: not only the 'end of Communism', but also the final petering out of the countercultural revolution, in which I had myself been swept up as a young adult. I think that the most useful way I can write here about *The Politics of Psychotherapy* – or, indeed, about the politics of psychotherapy – is to describe something of my own experience of 60s and 70s radicalism, and

---

2008. From a special feature on *The Politics of Psychotherapy* (Totton, 2006b) in *Psychotherapy and Politics International*.

then of the drastically changed climate of the 80s and 90s. It was during this transition that I became a therapist; and I think that many other therapists and therapeutic schools have been deeply marked by it.

Becoming a therapist

I spent the early 1970s, having graduated from Cambridge University, moving gradually leftward across the spectrum of radical politics until I eventually fell off the edge. Up to about 1972 I was in fact officially still part of the university, being registered, and receiving a grant, for a PhD in Renaissance literature, while living in London as a political activist and having contact with my supervisor once in a blue moon. Such was the difference of the times.

Over four years or so, I moved from involvement in the Haringey Free Press, a local alternative paper; to being part of the Tottenham Claimants Union, an organisation involving few claimants and few Tottenham residents, which I gradually discovered was a sort of front-cum-recruiting body for a 'proto-party group', two of whose leading members ended up serving long sentences in Northern Ireland; to joining the libertarian socialist squatting scene in Islington; to co-running Rising Free, a radical bookshop near Kings Cross; to co-founding Wicked Messengers, a post-situationist groupuscule squatting communally in South Hampstead ('If you cannot bring good news, then don't bring any').

The main thing that I gradually learnt over those four years is, in retrospect, simple and obvious, but at the time was terribly hard to grasp: that most people in this society do not want revolutionary social change, and therefore that revolutionary activism, generally speaking, is a mixture of hope, fantasy and manipulation. A defining moment was during a meeting of a North London libertarian socialist group. Some members had been researching a possible mass squat; they had found an empty block of flats and worked out how to gain access. After a congratulatory pause, someone said 'OK, now all we need is to find some homeless families'.

This and other similar experiences gradually moved me out of direct activism (at which I was never very good) and into the situationist orbit (Gray, 1974/1988; Plant, 1992). After all, May 68 was a defining experience of my life, even in the diluted Cambridge University version (occupations, but no tear gas, clubs or Molotovs); and situationist ideas and tactics were central to May 68. Perhaps people could be teased, provoked and subverted into revolutionary awareness.

Our main impact, I am afraid, was on the libertarian socialist left. (We invented an imaginary revolutionary group called Big Fist, and issued what were intended to be absurd communiqués. Several people tried to join, and were very annoyed to find out that they had been – inadvertently – taken in. The big fist nearly came in our direction.) Meanwhile our own lifestyle was being transformed, primarily by LSD, the logical next step (or so it seemed at the time) in an exploration of the potential for human liberation and the causes of human imprisonment.

Although acid taught me an enormous amount, it failed to do the job – or at any rate, to do the particular job I had set for it, of showing the path to revolution; and eventually I took refuge in North Yorkshire from a classic 70s welter of painfully confused relationships. On the kitchen wall of the shared cottage to which I moved was a flyer for a weekend workshop of Reichian therapy. Wilhelm Reich had been an iconic figure in the political scenes through which I moved, mainly for his utopian vision of a world governed by 'love, work and knowledge'; somehow I had overlooked the fact that he was primarily a psychotherapist. Reader, I attended the workshop; the rest is history.

What this means in practice is, first of all, that I discovered in Reich's work what still seems to me to be one of the most concrete, comprehensive and practical programmes for radical social change that I have ever encountered (although this partly only demonstrates the weakness of the competition); and secondly, that I ended up training and practising as a psychotherapist. The milieu in which I did so was, of course, drastically different from the milieu of therapy in 2008: we charged a lot less money, for a start; most of the people who came to us did so because they wanted to grow and change, rather than because they were in particular trouble, anyway so far as they were aware; and none of us – in my little neck of the woods anyway – were in it for the money, or for a career. Our work as therapists was a direct extension of our social commitment, our desire to help change the world.

The form of Reichian work which I was taught (Totton & Edmondson, 2009; West, 1988) was firmly situated within the human potential movement, the best home which Reich's work could find after his expulsion from the International Psychoanalytic Association (Sharaf, 1983). When I undertook an MA in Psychoanalytic Studies several years later, I found out that Reich's work was really better understood as a development of psychoanalysis (Totton, 1998b). This dual allegiance meant that right from the start I was in some senses working both sides of the street, using psychoanalytic concepts within a humanistic style –

which was in some ways rather confusing until I developed a clearer perception of what was going on, but overall, I think, a considerable advantage: having more than one therapeutic model tends to aid creativity (Bollas, 2007: 7).

Therapy and politics

Having come into therapy from the direction I did, and being around for a relatively long time, has allowed me to watch the process of regulation and professionalisation with a very critical eye. Like many other practitioners of my generation, I have always understood therapy as a *social* practice, a means to a potential social end: realising in the 1970s that most people didn't want a revolution, I was led to explore the psychosocial reasons for this (as well as exploring my unconscious and neurotic reasons, alongside the conscious ones, for wanting a revolution myself). I saw therapy as a means of psychological liberation, a way of freeing up our energy for individual and collective creativity. This is pretty much how I still see it.

The advocates of professionalisation take a drastically different view. They treat therapy as an occupation rather than as a calling; and while this is an antidote to grandiosity, it is also a recuperation of therapy's potential for liberation. But in any case, an *occupation* is not a *profession*; to be a profession, we must necessarily align ourselves with mainstream social values and styles of proceeding. I have argued in several places (e.g. Chapter 16, this volume; Totton, 2000) that therapy is inherently subversive of mainstream values and conventions – even, I think, when practised by people who see themselves as quite mainstream. However, making serious money out of therapy in proper post-80s style means marketing it as a mainstream profession, which seems to involve buying into the medical model of 'mental health provision'.

So, when invited by Open University Press to edit this book, I wanted to collect material that would help make all these points: about the inherent radicalism of the practice of psychotherapy; about therapy as 'politics carried out by other means'; about the potential uses of therapy as a means of understanding and addressing social problems; and about the distortion involved in treating therapy as just another profession. I think that the book does successfully argue and illustrate these points, and that some of the critical responses to it have been made exactly because it does.

I have said in several places, including the Introduction to and Chapter 7 of *The Politics of Psychotherapy* (Totton, 2006d, a), that psychotherapy is intrinsically and inevitably political. The view, reiterated by critics of the book, that psychotherapy should not concern itself with the social causes of distress is still *political:* a view not just of therapy, but implicitly of citizenship (that individual members of a society should leave politics to the 'experts') and also of life itself (that people suffer because of chance, their personal makeup, human nature, original sin, or some combination of these, rather than through the effects of the socio-political context).

Conservative political stances in all areas of life tend to present themselves as 'non-political'. Since they support the status quo (or, sometimes, what until recently was the status quo), they can argue for the inherent naturalness of things as they are, without exploring how they came to be so and in whose interests. This is effectively a trick: the belief that the current situation is one to be approved and encouraged is as political as its opposite. As George Orwell said in a different context in 1946, 'The opinion that art should have nothing to do with politics is itself a political attitude' (Orwell, 1946: 4). Speaking specifically of psychotherapy, at certain points its job has been generally agreed to be supporting the status quo and helping clients adjust to it (for instance, in the USA in the 1950s); and at other points, sometimes very close in time (for instance, in the USA in the 1960s), its job has been generally agreed to be challenging the status quo and helping clients resist it. What makes the difference is the socio-political context, which, in this example, psychotherapy clearly influenced through the human potential movement, but *by* which its view of its own task was shaped.

Now the wheel has turned again, and increasingly psychotherapy and counselling are expected to act as part of the security/surveillance society – the therapist as CCTV camera, 'for your safety and convenience'. This is not quite a return to the 50s: there are newer and even more worrying values at work. In 50s America, the required link between normative social values and therapeutic practice was at least openly spelt out. Now this link is deeply concealed behind a social rhetoric of diversity, but operates at the heart of concepts like 'safety' – for whom? – and 'evidence-based practice' – evidence of what, and by whose definition? The reality that therapy is a practice with risk and danger at its core, and which proceeds by informed guesswork and intuition, must be suppressed from public discourse.

However, whereas in the 1950s there was only very limited and marginal resistance to the hegemonic interpretation of the therapist's task – the therapeutic 'old left' having been decimated and demoralised by European fascism (R Jacoby, 1986) – there is now a considerable, articulate and well-organised opposition to the new hegemony. The values and self-descriptions which therapy worked out in the 60s and 70s, in response to massive social change (some of the most influential writings are Laing 1967; Cooper, 1976; Wyckoff, 1976; Rogers, 1978; Ernst & Goodison, 1981; Steiner, 1981; Guattari, 1984), have become deeply anchored in its being, largely through the influence of a whole generation of therapists who, like myself, cut their teeth in this period and went on to teach, supervise and write.

Conclusion

Psychotherapy is suffused with political judgements. It is also a field of political *action*, a place where power is exercised and contested, as therapists try to affect clients' lives, and clients acquiesce, resist, or do both at the same time (Totton, 2006a). At the same time, clients' problems can only fully be understood within a wider socio-political context, in which various forces are similarly trying to affect their lives while they acquiesce, resist, or both. Hence therapy may have something useful to say about how these two contexts, of society and individual life, relate.

It is clear that there is something in human culture which matches Marx's unsatisfactory dichotomy between 'base' and 'superstructure'. Individuals do correspond, in however complex a way, to the conditions set by the ensemble of social relations. But it is not easy to adequately describe this crucial correspondence. If we look at psychotherapy from this angle, we can see that it constitutes an ongoing research programme, using both historical reconstruction and here-and-now investigation, of the workings of families, their micropolitics, the processes through which children develop in certain directions and styles, the resistance as much as the acquiescence which forge subjectivity. This is not usually understood as political science! But, among other things, that is what it is.

Therapy involves itself centrally with the family, the field within which infants become adults, 'the place where psychic structure is formed' (Poster, 1978). The pioneering work of Wilhelm Reich (1933/1975) mapped out how family constellations give rise to character structure, conceived essentially as a relationship to power, an internalisation of social institutions. Psychotherapy charts also the *externalisation* of *psychic* structures, which forms those social institutions: a mutual, dialectical co-arising of individual and society.

As I wrote in *The Politics of Psychotherapy*:

> Mutuality, in fact, is the keynote of the relationship between psychotherapy and politics. One can sum it up as follows: *Psychotherapy and politics each problematize the other, and each contribute to solving problems which the other faces.* For example, politics identifies difficulties with the therapeutic project which we would often rather not consider – issues like discrimination, prejudice, domination, and hierarchy; while psychotherapy shows politics its own unconscious – the structures of projection and identification which scaffold it, the 'motivational and affective bases of political action' (Hoggett, 2004: 80). Politics shows how the roles of both client and therapist are socially constructed (Gergen, 1994), and how therapy constitutes a regulatory discourse of social control (Foucault, 1980). Therapy responds that something crucial is missing from this picture – the actual suffering of the subject, and the therapist's response to it.
>
> (Totton, 2006d: xvii)

The mutual friction between therapy and politics uncovers some of the deepest paradoxes in human experience, for example, the status of the self. Nikolas Rose (1990) suggests that the emphasis on personal responsibility in most therapy is a form of interpellation (Althusser, 1971) which pressures the client to take on a particular form of subjectivity. At the same time, though, therapy constantly and profoundly challenges this appearance of self-responsibility (see Chapter 12, this volume), most directly through the very notion of unconscious process, which also throws into question all the appearances of social and political life.

The Politics of Psychotherapy is not the last word on any of these issues – new thoughts are bursting out of me as I write this piece. But it seems to me a useful and significant step along the way to fully clarifying our thoughts about these matters.

Part 4
Ecopsychology and Embodiment

21

Embodied Relating

I want to talk about embodiment; and about relationship. In particular, I want to talk about the intimate relationship between the two. The specific style of body psychotherapy which I practice and teach is called Embodied-Relational Therapy, or ERT. In ERT we study the different ways in which humans try to deal with the problematic situation of being a body, and their implications for our life. However, focusing on our embodiment reveals that it cannot be separated from relationship.

Because we are embodied beings, our whole lives revolve around our need for relationship. To be a body is to need other bodies. We come into the world with our lives literally depending on our ability to form relationships with the adults around us, and with an innate passionate wish and capacity to do so – infants as young as 42 *minutes* will try to imitate adult expressions (Meltzoff & Moore, 1995). Far from the old paradigm of babies starting out merged with their mothers and only gradually differentiating, it becomes increasingly apparent that babies are born immediately *into* I–Thou relating; so that the self is created out of relationship with the other (Stern, 1985). The notion of merging turns out to be a wishful fantasy rather than an original reality.

This intense, eager readiness to relate that we find in infants is biologically rooted – grounded in our embodiment. It is a body-to-body relationship of skin, smell, eyes, mouth, which gradually becomes also mind to mind. In distinguishing these two, body and mind, I am only differentiating *aspects* of the human being, facets of our manifestation which can never actually be separated from each other. As Gregory Bateson (1979) says, 'mind' is inherent in the relationship of brain, body and environment.

As babies, and equally as adults, our most profound desire is for the Other, for the embodied pleasure, satisfaction and transcendence which connection with the Other can (in reality or in fantasy) provide. At the same time, we ourselves represent the

---

2007. A talk given at the BACP Annual Conference.

Other for other people; and the web of mutual need and desire can become very twisted indeed. We grow up *needing* relationship, and *fearing* it – fearing the uncontrollable, which we locate most painfully in our bodies and in our relationships. Embodied-Relational Therapy explores the possibility of relaxing into embodied relating.

The capacity to relax and to relate is what is being healed in most therapeutic encounters. Because of the difficulties we encounter in infancy and childhood, many of us end up with a sense of tension, or even opposition, between these two states, relaxing and relating. It can feel as though we have to choose one: being in relationship meets deep needs, but also creates deep anxieties about loss of control and often seems anything but relaxing. I think, though, that we all carry a dream, and are born with a potential, of relaxing deeply *and* relating deeply. Somewhere we know that 'control' is always an illusion born of fear, and that accepting our lack of control actually and paradoxically leads to a radical lessening of anxiety.

The capacity to relax and relate is embodied and – literally – innate, we are born with it. Like many human capacities, though, it needs to be *elicited* – stimulated and drawn out of us – and this eliciting is time-sensitive; the development of relatedness depends on having specific encounters at specific developmental moments. This is a good basic model for therapy, it seems to me: a collaboration between therapist and client to identify developmental launch windows which have not fully succeeded, and to generate some ability to repair that relational damage. All of this work of collaboration, research and repair is conducted *through the embodied therapeutic relationship*.

My suggestion is that we do this whether or not we are aware of it – in effect, we are all body psychotherapists, consciously or unconsciously. Because if the work is not done on the level of embodiment, it is not done at all. There is a good deal of current neuroscience research which indicates how this might work. First of all, though, I need to say that my view of therapy would be more or less the same without the input from neuroscience. Experience comes first, and my experience as a body psychotherapist is compelling; if neuroscience contradicted it, I would look for the problem first of all in neuroscience. However, the actuality is that neuroscience over recent years has confirmed the positions of body psychotherapy in the most extraordinary and compelling way.

Neuroscience offers us a set of what are in effect very useful, powerful metaphors for thinking about what happens in therapy. If we take those metaphors too literally, they can become unhelpful. For example, most neuroscientists put great emphasis on the *brain*, as if that was where all the action takes place. Some therapists have taken over this viewpoint, and talk as if therapy is a brain-to-brain operation between therapist and client, rather than a body-to-body one.

However, there are some significant neuroscience texts which make it clear that, as Roz Carroll (2002) has said, paralleling Winnicott's epigram that there is no baby without a carer, *there is no brain without a body* – because the brain is a specialised body organ where the body is *represented*. The well-known work of Antonio Damasio (e.g. 1996, 2000) asserts that the brain primarily represents the body through emotions. Along with several other writers, Damasio argues that emotions – which are intrinsically embodied phenomena – are our most effective way of processing input from the environment, our best way of thinking. And some of the neuroscience metaphors emphasise that our awareness is *distributed through our body*, rather than focused in our brain.

To experience ourselves as a brain on top of a body is a key form of dissociation, a version of the split between 'mind' and 'body': it is one of the problems which body therapy in particular tries to address. Winnicott argued very long ago that 'erratic mothering' can lead to an apparent opposition between what he called 'mind' and 'psyche-soma', since the baby tries to 'mother' itself by a process of dissociative splitting (Winnicott, 1949/1992).

To return to my main theme, then: neuroscience has a lot to say about the nature of human relating, about attachment and social bonding, and about the sorts of experiences in infancy and childhood which damage our capacity to form bonds of relationship. For example, neuroscience has recently identified what are known as 'mirror neurons' (e.g. Pineda, 2009): areas of the brain which fire *in response to actions which we see other people perform*, and so in effect mirror those actions in our own embodied being. Hence these mirror neurons are thought to be related to our capacity for empathy and for social behaviour, since they enable us to identify with the Other. More recently, mirror neurons have been found to fire in response to a *verbal description* of physical actions (Aziz-Zadeh et al, 2006). In a way this is an example of 'well, duh' research: we know that some such mechanism must exist, since we know that we can identify and empathise in this way.

I want to briefly describe another piece of neuroscience which I find particularly relevant; it's a little complicated, so please bear with me, I think it's worth it. Stephen Porges' Polyvagal Theory (1995, 1997, 2005) offers a new interpretation of the autonomic nervous system, the brain/body system which is outside conscious control. Porges looks at one branch of a cranial nerve called the vagal nerve, a major part of the parasympathetic side of the autonomic system. The branch on which he focuses works to calm and relax the heart. He shows that, although the vagal system is primarily about calming things down, this branch can actually be used as a flexible and controllable way to rapidly stimulate the heart and the metabolism in general, by *lessening* its action: if the vagal nerve is *less* activated, the heart will work *harder*. This offers a much gentler and more flexible alternative to the sympathetic system's adrenalin-based way of activating the metabolism, which floods us with stimulation and leaves us exhausted.

So the vagal nerve provides a way of energising ourselves to act in the world while not entering into survival-mode, fight–flight ways of processing events. In other words, it is a precise tool for social interaction. Instead of an on–off switch, it is adjustable, like a tap: we can have precisely the level of activation appropriate to the situation, and adjust this as the situation changes. Under normal circumstances, the sympathetic nervous system will only get activated if this vagal system is not working properly – like using a sledgehammer to crack a nut because the nutcrackers are broken.

Porges points out that this branch of the vagal nerve is one of several cranial nerves which all originate in the same area of the brain, an area which, in our early aquatic ancestors, was concerned with the function of the gills. If we put together the operation of all these cranial nerves, we get a very interesting picture. Some of them are still concerned with breath, and also with sucking, swallowing, salivation and vocalisation – in other words, with all the mechanisms which allow first of all breast feeding without suffocation, and then eventually articulate speech. Others let us tense the muscles of the middle ear, creating the ability to pick out and discriminate the frequencies of speech from the hum of background noise. Others control the expressive muscles of the face, and the muscles of the eyelids, so that they influence eye contact. All in all, this is an elaborate and subtle system for interrelating with other people, first as infants and then as adults: a system developed over evolutionary time by co-opting and synthesising pre-existing anatomy and physiology for new purposes. This sort of process is known as 'exaptation' – using a feature which evolved for one purpose to do something else altogether.

So Porges is describing a complex interactive network of cranial nerves and functional systems which was originally concerned with absorbing oxygen from water; gradually developed in mammals into a system for absorbing food and comfort from the mother's breast; and then, in humans, brought this together with visual and vocal interaction with our carer, becoming in adults a system for absorbing relational nourishment from our social context. And what is particularly pleasing for me as a body psychotherapist is that the whole system – what Porges calls the Social Engagement System – is focused on the *heart*, on the ability of good nourishing relating to calm and soften the heart. The theory offers neuroscientific backing for the experience of *heart-to-heart contact*.

I'd like to invite you to experiment with the Social Engagement System, by turning to a neighbour and interacting for a couple of minutes, absorbing some relational nourishment while tracking the involvement of your heart. See whether you can feel your heart responding and lifting in reaction to the connection you are establishing.

If you did notice a contactful response here, I suggest that it is at least partly because you were focused on internal, embodied experience, as well as external perception – external perception came together with proprioception, so that you were operating in three dimensions (3D). Working with the Social Engagement System represents a side of body psychotherapy which is about consulting the embodied self. In a very wide sense, I think it is true to say that awareness of embodiment shifts the therapy relationship from 2D to 3D: suddenly, instead of a flat encounter of mind-to-mind, there is a three-dimensional space in the room, filled with complex intensities, densities, currents and thresholds, movements and impulses to move.

Contact is the traditional way in which body psychotherapy talks about all this – a different metaphor. Contact is vital to the healing space: people are *in touch*, and energy flows between them. Our most primal experience of this is in the womb, surrounded and supported by fluid, with nourishment and information flowing directly into us through the umbilical cord. After birth, we need to remake that connection, through skin, eyes, ears, mouth, heart, energy field, bodily and verbal communication; and throughout life every relationship is partly a replay of this original contact. We need contact in order to live; and our primary model of contact, however abstract it may become, is a bodily one.

We also all have experiences of difficult contact, difficult connection, difficult energy, difficult feeding, which can make us very reluctant to open up to someone else. We may have to spend a lot of time in therapy – hours, weeks, years – working around contact: it is useless and dangerous to do any other work if living contact is not there. So establishing contact can easily become the whole of therapy with a particular person; and recognising contact and its absence, and different styles of resistance to contact, are key therapeutic skills.

Contact is importantly different from some other kinds of relating; three of these are worth identifying.

Merging

Womb experience is perhaps more like this: with no clear boundaries between us and the universe, we are part of the whole, floating in a sea of bliss. Everyone needs to dissolve like this sometimes – through sex, love, meditation, worship, time in nature, sleep. But losing boundaries needs to be voluntary, rather than being overwhelmed, flooded, seduced. And we need to *have* boundaries in the first place: some people are still trying to separate themselves off fully, to learn where they stop and the world starts.

Penetration

One way of reaching someone is to come inside their being. Some qualities of penetration – assertiveness, passion, demand – can be valuable aspects of contact. Some people sometimes can only be reached through insisting. As therapists, though, we have to learn to approach someone's boundary, and stop. Many people have had terrifying experiences of feeling invaded, abused, shattered, poisoned, which may derive from sexual, physical or mental abuse, from horrific births and other traumatic experiences, or from more chronic long-term relationships and atmospheres. This is different from involuntary merging: here instead of having weak or absent boundaries, the person has brittle, rigid, over-defined boundaries; they are cut off from contact through their fear of invasion.

Separateness

While some people are trying to separate themselves off, others are stuck in a separateness which they cannot overcome, leading to a lonely, isolated life. Just as losing our boundaries needs to be voluntary, *having* boundaries also needs to be voluntary.

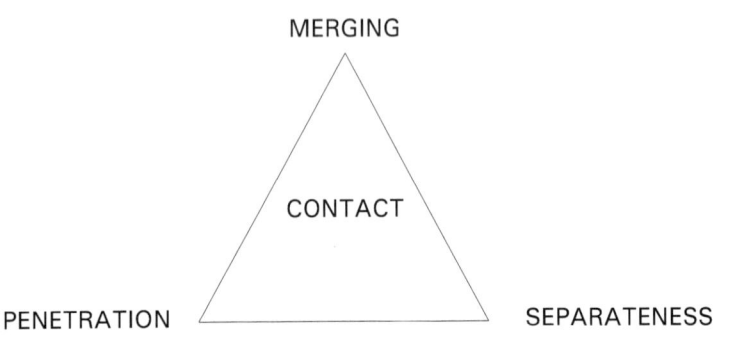

```
                    MERGING
                      /\
                     /  \
                    /    \
                   / CONTACT
                  /        \
                 /          \
   PENETRATION  /_____\  SEPARATENESS
```

These three qualities, merging, penetration and separateness, are all distinct from contact, yet related to it; at different times we need a flavour of each in order to improve our contact with someone. With each person we meet therapeutically, we have to sense their issues around contact, and find a way of building trust, forming relationship, allowing energy to flow safely between us. For some people, the fear is mainly of invasion or flooding; for others it's about lack of connection. Some believe they have to hide their insides because others will reject them; some feel they have to manipulate others or smash their defences in order to preserve themselves. Another sort of person plays constantly with contact and separation, advance and retreat.

Contact happens not only *between* people; it happens *within* a person, and between them and their environment. Grounding is a form of contact, and so is what ERT calls 'skying', contact with the cosmos and with spirit. We need contact with ourselves, with other people, and with our environment; all three depend on our capacity to tolerate spontaneity, to give up some control, to let the boundaries of our identity become relaxed and porous while still remaining comfortable about what is 'me' and what isn't. All this depends on our embodiment, which decides our ability to contact our own feelings, sensations, impulses, thoughts and fantasies. These give us most of our information about what is going on in the relationship field. Being in touch with ourselves, the world, and other people is modelling for our clients the possibility of living in a more relaxed and flexible way.

The key is to offer contact consistently, without invading or overriding the person's 'keep off' signals. Sometimes these are enormously easy to spot; but others find it very hard to say 'No', and have no belief that others will stay out. We need to be alert to and respectful of any feeling of hesitancy, resistance. Sometimes in therapy circles 'resistance' is spoken of as if it is a bad way to behave, something to overcome. But if we think of it in the sense of resistance to oppression, or resistance to infection, we may be able to support people's need to protect their integrity.

At the same time, though, it is necessary to offer contact, in a convincing and authentic way, which means above all working on our own resistance to and avoidance of contact, giving ourselves just as much respect and support as we do our clients, but finding our way through to a place where we can genuinely want to be with the other person. Times when we don't may tell us about what is going on for them as well as for us: our impatience or repugnance may mirror their negative expectation.

An important aspect of Stephen Porges' Social Engagement System theory is its focus on the biological conditions which allow human social bonding. As Porges says,

> social behaviors associated with nursing, reproduction, and the formation of strong pair bonds require a unique biobehavioral state characterized by immobilization without fear, and immobilization without fear is mediated by a co-opting of the neural circuit regulating defensive freezing behaviors through the involvement of oxytocin.
>
> (Porges, 2005: 33)

This unique state, which Porges says is required for nursing babies, for sex and for love, is also, of course, a requirement for effective psychotherapy: we need to be able to stay relaxed together in a state of intimacy. Porges is discussing a process of 'exaptation' – a parasympathetic system for defensive freezing has been developed into a way to relax and stay in contact even under strong stimulus – something of obvious relevance to psychotherapy. One of the things which attracts me about the Social Engagement System theory is that it represents a move on from attachment theory, with its focus on mother–infant relationships, to a theory of *social bonding*, of adult–adult relationship, which builds on infant attachment but transforms it into a peer interaction.

Whatever resources of expertise we bring to bear on body psychotherapy, drawing either from neuroscience or from other forms of skill and knowledge, it remains still and always an interpersonal, intersubjective process. The great contribution of body psychotherapy to therapy as a whole is its profound sense of how *embodied* intersubjectivity really is – and of how a person's style of embodiment defines their style of intersubjectivity, and vice versa. Bodies in relationship can generate an authenticity of contact that carries its own authority, and that grounds psychotherapy in ways which allow creative transformation. If we think of body psychotherapy as occurring in the unique relationship formed between two embodied subjects, neither of whose experience is privileged over that of the other, then we can see that among other functions it can be profoundly reparative.

So what am I suggesting that body psychotherapy can contribute to general therapeutic practice? Primarily, two things. Firstly, all therapists can benefit from being aware of their own state of embodiment, or lack of it. The more we are present in our bodies, in the room, with the client, the more use we can be: the more available we are to enter into relationship. And equally importantly, our bodies receive a high proportion of the messages that our clients emit about their own state of being. If we are not present in our bodily experience, this information will pass us by.

Secondly, therapists need to offer and accept contactful relationship with the client, not reject it. I was recently reminded how important this issue is on a workshop that I was leading. I was working face to face with a member of the group, and she was talking about her low self-esteem, and her feeling of being unattractive to men. I fed back to her my authentic experience in that moment of being very attracted by her energy and her physical being. The outcome of the piece of work was very positive for the woman; but afterwards another member of the group queried my response, and asked me whether I wasn't 'colluding with a neurotic need'. My spontaneous response was 'The need for relationship is not neurotic – it's a healthy need which should be supported not rejected.'

We need to be able to *meet* the demand for embodied contact which often starts to pour out of our clients as the work proceeds. By 'meeting' I don't necessarily mean physical contact – although personally I do often touch my clients, hug them, hold them, hold their hands or their heads. But there are other ways of holding: through words, of course, but words in themselves are sometimes, often, not enough – we need to hold through sparkling eye contact, through facial and bodily expression, through the spontaneous response of one embodied being to another. In the example I just gave, the *words* alone would not have been enough if my whole body had not been conveying the genuineness of my words.

Centrally, I think, we need to convey to our clients that *it is all right to be a body*. So many factors in our culture come together to deny this; to encourage us to split off from our embodiment, to identify as minds, as brains, as an illusion of control over the scary spontaneity of embodied existence. If we are to help our clients return to an identification with their bodily existence, and hence to a capacity for relaxed relating, then we need to be identified with our own bodies, and comfortable in them. This, I suggest, is the challenge that body psychotherapy offers to the rest of the therapy world.

22

Overwhelm

Ecological activists struggle with the question: Why do so many people ignore or deny information about climate change and general environmental collapse? If we are ourselves active around these issues, it is terribly easy to feel anger or contempt towards those who aren't, to see them as stupid and/or bad. But if we are going to address this disengagement effectively, we need to ask ourselves whether people might have very good reasons for adopting it. Ecopsychology – the study of human beings' psychological relationship with the other-than-human, and of what disturbs that relationship – has a great deal to contribute to understanding these reasons.

The one-word explanation for denial or avoidance is 'overwhelm'. Overwhelm operates on three levels. Firstly, there is overwhelm about the scale and complexity of the crisis: not only are the suggested outcome scenarios ghastly beyond belief (literally so for some), but the problems are all interlinked, and for every apparent solution someone points out new problems Just as ecosystemic elements themselves are profoundly interwoven, the same applies to ecosystemic damage. It is clear to anyone who looks that environmentalists are fire-fighting, running endlessly from emergency to emergency. After all, if aliens landed today and handed us a source of abundant non-polluting energy, we would still wake up tomorrow facing environmental disaster from a whole array of other causes.

But there is also overwhelm in each person's personal life. In advanced capitalist culture, nearly all of us are on the edge of being unable to cope, to do what we have to do and process what we have to process while also handling our internal emotional states. And a further level of this is cultural overwhelm, the result of many generations of trauma through war, famine, disease, and abuse. We are all deeply distressed and struggling to cope, and we bring this distress to environmental issues just as we do to everything else.

2010. Another editorial for *Psychotherapy and Politics International*, written after leading a seminar for a green activist organisation exploring why it is so difficult to move people to action.

Individuals seek to protect a fragile bubble of personal reality which makes their lives bearable. Some key elements of this are fun, freedom, status-based identity, and, most fundamentally, *relaxation*. Environmental activists seem to threaten all of these elements, which in many of their most common forms (consumption, travel, entertainment) involve high carbon levels. In particular, they threaten relaxation: the human need for downtime, empty mental space, periods when we are not anxious and planning for survival. Even if we can only get relaxation through getting drunk and watching TV, it is still deeply precious and we will protect it at all costs.

Hence, for large numbers of people it is not climate change itself which appears as a threat, but *news* of climate change, which threatens to break into their fragile bubble of emotional survival. They respond to this news as mammals respond to threat to survival: with the well-known triad of fight/flight/freeze. In particular, many people freeze: they use the response reserved for desperate situations where we are completely helpless, and our best option is to turn off, go into trance and hope to be overlooked.

This is what is also called *dissociation*. It is an important part of the mammalian repertoire, but one which gets drastically overused in modern urban environments, where we need it just to get through the morning rush hour. In some contexts, then, it is a healthy, pro-survival talent; but unfortunately not one which helps with the situation we are currently facing. In some ways climate change *deniers* are a better prospect for environmentalists than climate change *ignorers*: at least they are mobilised enough around the issue to fight the information rather than freeze or run away. (Activists, of course, are also using a 'fight' strategy to cope with overwhelm – which makes them vulnerable to collapse and burnout.)

Until people are willing and able to tolerate the feelings which environmental information sets off in them – feelings like fear, grief, rage, despair – it will be very difficult for them to absorb that information, and therefore to act on it. So how can we help them (and ourselves) to come out of overwhelm? The first thing to do when faced with overwhelm in a therapeutic situation is to point out to the person that this is what is going on: 'It's all a bit much, isn't it?' 'It's hard for you to take things in just now.' Just on its own, this helps people find some solid ground. Then we need to establish a sense of safety in which they can access their embodied emotions.

I would suggest that environmental activists need to think about ways in which they can use these same strategies: helping people become aware that they have, for very good psychological reasons, become overwhelmed and cut off; and then supporting the sense that it is safe and OK to feel what we feel. Only after that will anyone be ready to think and act.

23

Wild Therapy

More and more practitioners now are becoming aware of *ecopsychology*, the study of human beings' psychological relationship with the ecosystems of which we are a part, and *ecotherapy*, the application of these ideas to therapeutic practice; in fact *Therapy Today* has run several articles on these themes. Until quite recently, though, there hasn't been much close thinking about the relationship between ecological ways of thinking and feeling on the one hand, and therapy on the other. The tendency has been to bolt therapeutic ideas onto ecopsychology, or ecopsychological ideas onto therapy, without really bringing the two together into a new whole. Such a fusion is one purpose of my new book, *Wild Therapy* (Totton, 2011c).

In writing the book, I realised that in order for therapy to think and feel ecologically, it has to change some of its core attitudes. But paradoxically, I also found that the elements of an ecological therapy were already present in the field, often without being perceived as such. What I therefore tried to do in the book was to identify these implicit elements and assemble them in a coherent way, so as to describe a way of doing therapy which is new, but also always-already present – an ecosystemic therapy which recognises that humans don't stand alone in the universe, but are profoundly connected with and dependent on other species and entities with whom we share this earth; and recognises also that skilful living stems from a capacity for spontaneity and yielding to what is, rather than from a struggle to exert control over self and others.

The emphasis on spontaneity is as much part of ecological awareness as the emphasis on connectedness. Both ideas follow from systems theory, which sees the world as a set of complex, self-organising, adaptive systems, where nothing *causes* anything else in a linear sense, but everything mutually *responds* to everything else, in a way which corresponds closely to the Buddhist concept of *paticca samuppada*, 'dependent co-arising'. Hence trying to isolate oneself from the world and exercise control over it is ultimately self-defeating – as we are seeing with the current ecological crisis.

2011. Published in *Therapy Today*.

Therapy has generally stood against the dominant cultural message, 'Be in control of yourself and your environment': it has tried to help people tolerate the anxiety of not being in control – of our feelings, our thoughts, our body, our future. There has always been a struggle over this issue, however, as new forms of therapy constantly arise which claim 'You can be in control after all'. And currently the dominant social structure is saying that therapy itself must be controlled, brought within the field of surveillance, monitoring, regulation, safety. As the world becomes increasingly frightening, it becomes increasingly necessary to pretend that security can be achieved, through ever-greater monitoring, surveillance and censorship – and this process in turn ratchets up our fear and insecurity. This is the path our society seems to be taking; but equally, of course, it is an internal psychological process, embodying exactly the anxieties which therapy arose to address.

So why *Wild* Therapy? For me this is a powerful way of pointing out the ever-present tension in human culture between the wild and the domesticated. In the move from hunter-gatherer society to agriculture, human beings tried to gain control over the world, over each other, and over the other-than-human and more-than-human. In doing this we split ourselves off from the world – it became, in fact, our 'environment', rather than the whole, of which we are an integral part. In Ursula LeGuin's resonant phrase, we learnt to live 'outside the world' (LeGuin, 1988: 153). By trying to control the world we have made it *other,* and therefore dangerous and frightening. The more we seek control, the closer we seem to get to it, the further our goal recedes. As the *Tao Te Ching* tells us, the more we try to control things the further out of balance we push them:

> Do you think you can take over the universe and improve it?
> I do not believe it can be done.
> ...
> The world is ruled by letting things take their course.
> It cannot be ruled by interfering.
>   (Feng & English, 1972, Sections 29 and 48)

Therapy is by nature wild; but a lot of it at the moment is rather tame. The book is intended to help shift the balance back towards wildness, by showing how therapy can connect with ecological thinking, and hence with the mutual co-creation of all beings. When we think ecosystemically, we see each species, each being, each person, not as an isolated monad, a sort of old-fashioned billiard ball atom interacting with other billiard balls by knocking into them – but as inherently and profoundly linked with every other species, being, person. We develop a sense of the endless complexity of existence; and realise that wildness, a state where things are allowed to happen of their own accord, is far more deeply complex than domesticated civilisation, just as a jungle – or even a piece of wasteland – is more complex than a garden.

Although the path of control is becoming increasingly emphasised in society, it has been with us since the Neolithic development of domestication. This was not just about humans domesticating other species; we also and above all domesticated *ourselves*. Hence the subtitle of the book, 'Undomesticating inner and outer worlds'. How far can we reasonably hope to go in moving away from domestication, given that the sustainable forager population of the earth in the Palaeolithic era was perhaps around one person per square mile?

In a literal sense, we clearly cannot go very far at all. A reduction of humanity to Palaeolithic population levels – which a few people are desperate enough to hope for – will only happen through catastrophe; and only in this way could surviving humans live wild in the literal sense. In *Wild Therapy* I explore the possibility of developing a wildness which is less literal, but perhaps none the less real and important: a reconnection with what I describe as 'Wild Mind', which is necessarily at the same time a reconnection with the world and with the other beings which inhabit it – and this will involve living, as well as thinking and feeling, in very different ways. Wild Mind refers to a state of awareness in which humans will not *want,* or be prepared, to damage the world for our own short-term comfort and convenience.

Wild Therapy offers a context for all this through connecting the attitudes of forager cultures with contemporary Western understandings of consciousness, so as to delineate a mode of being present in *all* cultures (Wild Mind); it suggests how this can be expressed through a 'wild therapy', not newly invented, but bringing together a wide range of already-existing ideas and practices. Some features I propose for wild therapy are:

- It recognises the interdependence of everything that exists.
- It is through-and-through relational.
- It identifies the role of the other-than-human and more-than-human in the therapeutic process.
- It supports, protects and defends liminality.
- It celebrates embodiment as a central aspect of our existence.
- It welcomes the spontaneous and the unknown, trusting what arises of its own accord.

- It seeks to transform fear-based defensive practice into undefensive, contact-based, adventurous practice.

As I have stated, all of these features are present in the therapy field already; but I think it makes an important difference to identify and connect them in this way, and to show how they involve an ecological way of understanding.

So *Wild Therapy* looks in one direction towards therapeutic practice; and in another direction towards the 'deep background' of human nature and human history. It also looks in a third direction, and asks how therapy can contribute to changing our relationship with the ecosystem of which we are part. To avoid environmental catastrophe, the world needs a change of heart, a fundamental shift of consciousness and behaviour which is perhaps only slightly less hard to imagine than a return to a hunter-gatherer lifestyle. However, it is necessary; without it, a literal return to hunter-gatherer life (and population levels) may be the *best* we can hope for. I believe psychotherapy and counselling have an important role to play in supporting and facilitating Wild Mind, or ecological consciousness. Changes of heart are what therapy specialises in; and ever since it began, therapy has been trying to help the world change its heart, by offering it collective as well as individual therapy. The only problem, as Andrew Samuels points out, is that like many individual clients who at first seem enthusiastic, 'the world has not shown up for its first session. The world is ambivalent about its therapy, suspicious of its political therapists, reluctant to be a patient' (Samuels, 1993: 30).

This isn't hard to explain. Most people are deeply traumatised, acutely or sub-critically, personally and/or by inheritance, and live in a society which as a whole is also traumatised; trauma gives rise to dissociation and denial. I trace this trauma to its origins, mythical or otherwise, in what I call the Neolithic bargain, when we exchanged the freedom and well-being of a hunter-gatherer lifestyle for the combination of protection from other humans and increasingly damaged attachment which goes along with urban existence in patriarchal societies. The structures of domination which this created now reach very deeply into our psyches and bodies; in viral fashion, they seek to take over and control every new social formation that arises. As we are currently experiencing, they make it enormously hard for us to free our attention to deal with the environmental crises we face. In advanced capitalist culture, nearly all of us are on the edge of being unable to cope, unable to do what we have to do and process what we have to process while also handling our internal emotional states. And a further level of this is *cultural* overwhelm, the result of many generations of damage through war, famine, disease, and abuse. We are all deeply distressed and struggling to cope; and we bring this distress to environmental issues just as we do to everything else.

This applies equally to collective overwhelm around climate change and other environmental disasters. If people feel threatened by the *news* of danger, then redoubling our efforts to spread the news will actually be counterproductive. As 'therapists to the world', we need to find ways of helping people become aware that they are in overwhelm, under the bedclothes with their fingers in their ears. We also need a parallel strategy of helping people reconnect with their innate love and awe for the other-than-human and the more-than-human, so that they start to feel revulsion against their mistreatment.

These strategies are supportive rather than aggressive; in tune with the human capacity for Wild Mind, rather than driving it underground. However, they are hard to apply in a situation which screams 'EMERGENCY' as soon as we let it into our consciousness. And, of course, change is not only a matter of individual or even collective consciousness. There are huge structures of power and money which necessarily oppose the wilding of the world, because any such process will destroy them. We may despise political leaders for their inaction around climate change, but few of them are fools: they know that capitalism can only survive through constant expansion, and that the consequences if capitalism abruptly fails would be disastrous – for humans at least – on a level similar to the consequences of climate change.

I believe that Wild Therapy has a role to play in the doubtful and difficult work of creating a new culture which can live well on the earth without damaging ourselves and other beings. There are many enormous obstacles to this work, and it isn't easy to see how it can succeed; it will involve remaking our economic system, and abandoning structures of domination and hierarchy which have been in place for millennia. Fortunately, though, *things will happen of their own accord*, as newly emergent features of the complex web of being, not following any intention or plan. If a new culture is going to come into existence, then it must be already brewing, already cooking in many thousands of places around the planet; slowly assembling itself out of millions of local acts of creativity and resistance. This may not be enough; but we can relax in the knowledge that it will be as good as it is possible for it to be. If we can accept this, it comforts us, stops us wasting our time trying to control the future, and at the same time shows us our path, which is to *envision* and *live* the future we desire.

24

The Body in the World, the World in the Body

We now have the means to exert an unprecedented degree of control over bodies, yet we are also living in an age which has thrown into radical doubt our knowledge of what bodies are and how we should control them.
(Chris Shilling, *The Body and Social Theory*)

Like most therapies, body psychotherapy has traditionally been concerned with what happens in one person and one body. In this article, following new trends in the field, I want to go beyond the individual and explore two bodies together, or a room full of bodies, or a whole world full of bodies. I believe that to truly inhabit our bodies is an invaluable resource, for us as individuals, for therapeutic practice, and for the future of the planet.

We enter the world as bodies, primed to seek contact with other bodies. Babies start imitating the expressions and movements of other people within minutes of birth (Meltzoff & Moore, 1995: 49-50). For years from birth we are dependent for our survival on adult carers, and urgently need to attract and hold their attention. But this is an abstract way of describing what all carers for infants experience: the passionate and skilful delight babies find in creating embodied relationship, and the storms of grief and despair with which they respond to disturbances in relationship. Long before a baby can form anything describable as a thought, its bodymind is capable of complex and subtly intelligent interactions through gaze, expression, voice and movement (Stern, 1985; Trevarthen & Aitken, 2001). The precise history of each baby's relationship experiences shapes the adult's personality and their ability to bond with others.

Adult humans do horrible things to each other's bodies, and to their own. This is possible, I think, because they have previously experienced a process of *disembodiment*, through various traumas, which cuts them off from the reality of what they are doing, and

---

2012. The most recent piece in this collection, written for *Therapy Today* partly to publicise the European Association for Body Psychotherapy conference in Cambridge in September 2012.

from the relatedness we seek as babies (Prescott, 1975). Young men can kill and mutilate each other in war because they have been traumatised by their military training, and by many of their experiences growing up as boys: child soldiers in Africa only exaggerate what happens everywhere. Old men can send young men to be killed, because their own experiences – often including battle, and being sent away to boarding school – have numbed and distanced them, allowing them to substitute abstractions for reality. Soldiers around the world, including the West, brutalise, torture and rape noncombatants, something they can only do because they are disconnected from their embodied being. Some of the most shocking atrocities involve attacks on pregnant women, babies and unborn children – perhaps attacks by soldiers' hard, cruel adult identity upon their own soft baby self.

Disembodiment affects our lives in many less dramatic ways. It makes it possible for workers to spend their days in meaningless and unpleasant labour; for women and children to be sexually exploited by men; for men and women, boys and girls, to force their bodies to conform to gender stereotypes; for humanity as a species to systematically destroy its own physical environment, and the other-than-human species which make it up. It is the context in which anorexia, bulimia and obesity thrive; cosmetic surgery appears increasingly normal; many millions worldwide succumb to addictions of various kinds; and we have a worldwide 'epidemic' of depression, intensifying closer to the heartlands of Western culture.

The concept of disembodiment depends on *embodiment.* Body psychotherapists use 'embodiment' as a name for the moment-by-moment experience of our existence as living bodies, with all the joy and grief, pleasure and pain, power and vulnerability that involves. Embodiment is not a *state*, but an ongoing *process of becoming embodied*, more and more deeply committed to our corporeal experience. It challenges us to own and integrate the various woundings we encounter in life, rather than leaving them frozen in sets of bodily tensions and avoidances which create a blank spot in our awareness and sensitivity. The reality for each individual will always be a set of compromises, as our embodiment finds ways to make the best of its situation, to preserve as much freedom and flexibility as possible; and body psychotherapy tries to help clients explore and re-evaluate these bodily choices.

As well as our lived awareness of being bodies, 'embodiment' also refers to the bodily process of absorbing and enacting social and cultural reality. From this point of view, embodiment is a summation of how the body suffers, accommodates, and transmits an ensemble of social and cultural stresses and tensions, which often therefore appear as simply 'the way things are'. Embodiment in this sense can often suppress embodiment in the other sense, substituting an objectified perception of the body. In a culture largely alienated from embodied experience, there is an ongoing struggle between lived embodiment and the body as object, in which body psychotherapy has always been deeply involved. As Don Hanlon Johnson says:

> Underlying the various techniques and schools, one finds a desire to regain an intimate connect with bodily processes: breath, movement impulses, balance and sensibility. In that shared impulse, this community is best understood within a much broader movement of resistance to the West's long history of denigrating the value of the human body and the natural environment.
> (Johnson, 1997: xvi)

Women and other non-mainstream groups in Western society, for example, people of colour, have tended to be identified by the mainstream with feelings and bodies, and these have been devalued in comparison with reason and intellect. For many men identifying with their body and emotions feels 'unmanly'; for many women their alignment with body and emotions feels like the seal of their oppression. Body psychotherapists – indeed, all therapists and counsellors – necessarily have to address these issues in their work.

A related cultural theme is the 'consumerist body': the body as subject and object of consumption.

> In the current configuration of the market economy the body becomes a possession which, through its appearance, provides opportunities for social and professional advancement: appearance, display and the management of impression are the capital goods of the consumer economy.
> (Lyon & Barbalet, 1994: 51)

Lyon and Barbalet emphasise that the consumerist body 'is very much the body we have and do things to. ... The consumerist body is objectified in its relations to others' (ibid: 52). Women tend to bear the brunt of its demands, as it encourages us to experience our body as a passive object, almost an 'accessory' itself, something to be exploited just as the natural world is exploited – and also further marginalising the old, the unattractive, the disabled or unusual-looking, who cannot offer a valuable commodity to the market.

Two examples

I want now to show something of how I, as a body psychotherapist, encounter and respond to social and cultural issues expressed through my clients' embodiment; which may also, hopefully, encourage other therapists and counsellors to notice this dimension of experience. Not much in my work with these two clients is specific to body psychotherapy; only, perhaps, my sensitivity and attention to issues of embodiment.

When we as therapists are impacted by the client's embodiment, we directly experience in our embodied countertransference its compromises, its contradictions, how it is incorporated (literally!) into social narratives and also resists or evades such incorporation – all of this, for the length of the session, becomes part of our own lived embodiment, and resonates with our own multiplicity of compromises and contradictions. I want to give two examples from my practice (treated at more length in Totton, 2008), using composite and fictionalised case vignettes, of how through the body the world can enter the therapy room.

'Naomi' was anorexic, not quite to the point of life threat, and tending to exercise addiction. She was also very attractive, with enormous eyes, high cheekbones, and long legs: a beauty which teetered right on the edge of emaciation, so that my perception of her veered between desire, horror and protective tenderness. Naomi was Jewish; her grandmother had died in a concentration camp. Neither of us could separate her emaciation from this context.

Her 'attractiveness' in itself raised major questions. Attractiveness is not the objective quality it masquerades as, but specific to time, space and culture: like everyone, I have been trained by glossy magazines to perceive certain physical characteristics as attractive, and these characteristics are selected for complex reasons. There is currently intense social pressure on women to shape their bodies in conformity with an exaggeratedly slim norm. Naomi was tall; in her early teens, she had tended to fat. Her stepmother was a much-admired beauty.

This no doubt sketches a familiar enough picture. But what I struggled not to leave out of the picture was *my own investment* in Naomi's self-starvation: how much I might have been repelled by a fat version of her, and was stimulated by the doe-like fragility of her embodied self-representation. In the countertransference, I enacted the male gaze which demanded slimness – not only her father, whose appreciation she badly needed, but the collective male gaze of our culture.

Naomi was clever and sophisticated enough to understand all this. But by thinking cleverly with her about it all, I was also collaborating with her anorexic rejection of the body in favour of the mind – while still enjoying her visual presence. I experienced a bizarre double perception: rejecting and starving her body, Naomi was simultaneously creating a desirable artefact for my enjoyment, irrespective of her own libidinal emptiness. I came to dread our sessions.

The way forward that we found – an unsatisfactory compromise – involved my sharing with her many of my responses and fantasies, including the fantasy that our interaction was an erotic intimacy. This engendered in her a seed of rage which offered some new freedom within the structures constraining her – an alternative to self-starvation. We finished therapy at some emotional distance from each other; but Naomi was eating.

What we didn't address together was precisely the body-in-itself, supposedly the focus of body psychotherapy. In other words, we didn't work (much) with the infantile levels of experience, Naomi's early relationship with her mother, who died when she was seven. We privileged the Oedipal level, the little girl's painful response to what society required of her. How much did my own post-Oedipal requirement of her, partly drowning out my tender response to the infant, act as an obstacle to therapy – and how much did my countertransference accurately and usefully zero in on her primary issues?

I want to underline how hopeless it would have been to leave out the social dimension, and treat our work together as purely a matter of individual relating. Our therapeutic 'success' was partial and ambivalent; but I don't believe even this could have happened if I had been unable to place Naomi's difficulties, *and my own responses to her*, in the context of cultural values around women's thinness and fragility.

'Ken' brought a contrasting issue of embodiment: he was covered, on first impression, with piercings and tattoos, and wearing a spiky Mohican haircut and a punk kilt over his trousers. (Ken was in his late forties.) Once I was past this rather overwhelming sight, there were about twelve piercings, visible and hidden (including genital), tattoos on his neck and on each arm, and a large one on his back. Ken was a rather shy and quietly spoken man, and his main presenting issue was difficulty in handling the sort of public attention which his appearance created.

Naturally enough, I soon mentioned the contrast between his professed dislike of standing out and his chosen appearance. Ken tried to explain that I was missing the point. He was not 'attention-seeking,' but suffering from the fact that his expression of his core identity was unusual and often unacceptable to others. He sought help not in changing his appearance, but in handling other people's reactions.

Never having worked with someone from Ken's subculture before, it was helpful to think about a more familiar situation: a gay person at ease with their sexuality but suffering from other people's prejudice. It helped even more to think of a transvestite with parallel issues. It was not my job, it seemed to me, to embody society's difficulty with Ken's self-presentation, but to support him in his problematic situation, and see what emerged as trust developed between us.

The way I found to support him was, as so often, to be interested in his experience: asking him what his piercing and tattooing meant to him, the significance of the particular images inscribed on his body, and also, of course, what it felt like; my own mildly prurient curiosity was very useful here ('Did it hurt?'). I found out a great deal about not only Ken's individual take on body modification, but also the subculture of which he was part, what he called his 'tribe.'

From my experience with Ken, Sweetman (1999: 52-53) is right to call body modification 'a form of antifashion ... an attempt to lend corporeal solidity to expressions of individuality.' 'Individuality' here is a complex concept: people frequently use 'body mod' to express their individuality by looking similar to each other. I am not mocking this: I think that for Ken, like many others, there is a very real fulfilment in coming together with those who share his unusual taste in embodiment (something hugely facilitated by the Internet). Other people's body mod and appearance influenced him primarily through his recognition of something corresponding to his own desire.

It would have been crass to make the obvious interpretation that Ken's body mod was a compensation for his shyness. This shyness was only relative, and perhaps only noticeable by contrast with the perceptual 'loudness' of his appearance. More importantly, to think in terms of compensation would refuse validity to his body mod on its own terms, and hence frontally attack Ken's identity – equivalent to 'explaining' a client's gayness in terms of developmental deficit, while another client's heterosexuality passes without comment.

As it happens, Ken *was* gay; 20 years earlier people would no doubt have treated his sexual orientation similarly to how they now treated his body mod. And in another 20 years? Are 'early adopters' inherently deviant – or to put it differently, are social deviants inherently psychologically deviant? Personally, I often feel enormous admiration for the courage and skill of those who successfully negotiate a space for their deviant or 'perverse' embodiment, for what we might call, in more than one sense, their queerness (Totton, 2006e). Eventually, Ken and I did have useful conversations about the deep significances for him of piercing, wounding, penetrating, and scarring as one might explore the significances of any client's sexual expression; but only after we had clearly established that I was not treating these significances as the 'real,' 'fundamental' meaning of his embodiment style.

I am conscious of the force of my countertransference reactions to these two clients. The traditional way of processing this would have been to explore the internal roots of my response, to restore 'balance'; and then to address the various 'narcissistic' and other clinical issues being presented by the clients. Such an approach would be neither therapeutic nor realistic. To in any sense 'see through' socially conditioned versions of embodiment, we need to include, and indeed navigate by, our countertransference, rather than strive for some imaginary neutrality.

Conclusion

In this article I have only managed to look at a few of the issues around embodiment and the world, touching on an embodied version of attachment in infants and social bonding in adults – and on what can go badly wrong – and also exploring how relational body psychotherapy discovers the social in the personal. Other relevant themes include the contributions which body psychotherapy, and an embodied approach in general, could make to conflict resolution and the pursuit of social justice; and the crucial importance of embodiment for ecopsychology and for the development of a more sane relationship between human beings and the other-than-human.

References

Althusser, L (1971) Ideology and ideological state apparatuses. In *Lenin and Philosophy and Other Essays* (pp 127-87). London: New Left Books. Online at http://www.marx2mao.com/Other/LPOE70NB.html

American Psychiatric Association (1994) *Diagnostic and Statistical Manual of Mental Disorders* (4th ed). Washington, DC: Author.

Aron, L (2001) *A Meeting of Minds: Mutuality in psychoanalysis*. Hillsdale, NJ: The Analytic Press.

Audergon, A (2005) *The War Hotel: Psychological dynamics in violent conflict*. London: Whurr.

Aziz-Zadeh, L, Wilson, SM, Rizzolatti, G & Iacoboni, M (2006) Congruent embodied representations for visually presented actions and linguistic phrases describing actions. *Current Biology, 16*, 1-6.

Bates, Y & House, R (Eds) (2003) *Ethically Challenged Professions: Enabling innovation and diversity in psychotherapy and counselling*. Ross-on-Wye: PCCS Books.

Bateson, G (1973) *Steps to an Ecology of Mind*. London: Paladin.

Bateson, G (1979) *Mind and Nature: A necessary unity*. New York: Ballantine Books.

Beisser, A (1972) The paradoxical theory of change. In J Fagan & IL Shepard (Eds) *Gestalt Therapy Now* (pp 77-80). New York: Harper. Online at http://www.gestalt.org/arnie.htm

Berne, E (1968) *Games People Play*. Harmondsworth: Penguin.

Bion, WR (1988) Notes on memory and desire. In E Spillius (Ed) *Melanie Klein Today. Vol. 2: Mainly Practice* (pp 15-18). London: Routledge. (Original work published 1967)

Bion, WR (1992) *Cogitations*. London: Karnac.

Bloom, SL (2004a) Neither liberty nor safety: The impact of fear on individuals, institutions, and societies, Part I. *Psychotherapy and Politics International, 2*(2), 78-98.

Bloom, SL (2004b) Neither liberty nor safety: The impact of fear on individuals, institutions, and societies, Part II. *Psychotherapy and Politics International, 2*(3), 212-28.

Bollas, C (2007) *The Freudian Moment*. London: Karnac.

Buckingham, D (1998) Letter. *Counselling: The Journal of the British Association for Counselling, 9*(3), 175.

Cant, S & Sharma, U (1996) *Complementary and Alternative Medicines: Knowledge in practice*. London: Free Association Books.

Carroll, R (2002) *Embodiment and Emotion*. Seminar given for conference on April 16th 2002 at the Tavistock Centre, London.

Castoriadis, C (1999) The psychical and social roots of hate. *Free Associations*, 7(3), 402–15.

Cooper, A (2001) The state of mind we're in: Social anxiety, governance and the audit society. *Psychoanalytic Studies*, 3(3–4), 349–62.

Cooper, D (1976) *The Grammar of Living*. Harmondsworth: Penguin.

Cooper, M (2008) *Essential Research Findings in Counselling and Psychotherapy: The facts are friendly*. London: Sage.

Damasio, A (1996) *Descartes' Error: Emotion, reason and the human brain*. London: Papermac.

Damasio, A (2000) *The Feeling of What Happens: Body, emotion and the making of consciousness*. London: Heinemann.

Davies, D & Charles, N (1996) *Pink Therapy: Guide for counsellors working with lesbian, gay and bisexual clients*. Maidenhead: Open University Press.

Davies, JM (2004) Whose bad objects are we anyway? Repetition and our elusive love affair with evil. *Psychoanalytic Dialogues*, 14(6), 711–32.

Denman, C (2003) *Sexuality: A biopsychosocial approach*. London: Palgrave Macmillan.

Doi, T (2002) *The Anatomy of Dependence: The key analysis of Japanese behavior*. London: Kodansha International Ltd.

Eichenbaum, L & Orbach, S (1983) *Understanding Women: A feminist psychoanalytic perspective*. New York: Basic Books.

Elliot, M, Bishop, K & Stokes, P (2004) Societal PTSD? Historic shock in Northern Ireland. *Psychotherapy and Politics International*, 2(1), 1–16.

Epstein, RS & Simon, RI (1990) The exploitation index: An early warning indicator of boundary violations in psychotherapy. *Bulletin of the Menninger Clinic*, 54, 450–65.

Ernst, S & Goodison, L (1981) *In Our Own Hands: A book of self-help therapy*. London: The Women's Press.

Feng, G-F & English, J (1972) *Lao Tsu: Tao Te Ching*. Aldershot: Wildwood House.

Ferenczi, S (1999) Confusion of tongues between adults and the child (the language of tenderness and of passion). In J Borossa (Ed) *Ferenczi: Selected writings* (pp 293–303). London: Penguin. (Original work published 1933)

Ferenczi, S (1999) The problem of the termination of the analysis. In J Borossa (Ed) *Ferenczi: Selected writings* (pp 245–54). London: Penguin. (Original work published 1927)

Foucault, M (1980) *Power/Knowledge: Selected interviews and other writings 1972–1979*. New York: Pantheon.

Frank, JD (1973) *Persuasion and Healing*. Baltimore, MD: Johns Hopkins University Press.

Freud, S (1912) Recommendations to physicians practising psycho-analysis. *Standard Edition*, Vol XII (pp 109–20). London: Hogarth Press.

Freud, S (1913) On beginning the treatment (further recommendations on the technique of psycho-analysis I). *Standard Edition*, Vol 12 (pp 121–44). London: Hogarth Press.

Freud, S (1926a) The question of lay analysis. *Standard Edition*, Vol XX (pp 177–258). London: Hogarth Press.

Freud, S (1926b). Inhibitions, symptoms and anxiety. *Standard Edition*, Vol XX (pp 75–175). London: Hogarth Press.

Fromm, E (1960) *The Fear of Freedom*. London: Routledge and Kegan Paul. (Original work published 1942)

Geertz, C (1973) Thick description: Toward an interpretive theory of culture. In *The Interpretation of Cultures: Selected Essays* (pp 3–30). New York: Basic Books.

Geertz, C (1983) *Local Knowledge: Further essays in interpretive anthropology*. New York: Basic Books.

Geller, L (1982) The failure of self-actualization theory: A critique of Carl Rogers and Abraham Maslow. *Journal of Humanistic Psychology, 22*, 56–73.

Gennino, A (Ed) (1990) *Amazonia: Voices from the rainforest*. San Francisco: Rainforest Action Network and Amazonia Film Project.

Gergen, K (1994) *Realities and Relationships: Soundings in social construction*. Cambridge, MA: Harvard University Press.

Giddens, A (1991) *Modernity and Self Identity*. Oxford: Polity Press.

Gitelson, M (1989) Theoretical problems in the analysis of normal candidates. In RF Lax (Ed) *Essential Papers on Character Neurosis and Treatment* (pp 409–27). New York: New York University Press. (Original work published 1954)

Glendinning, C (1994) *My Name is Chellis and I'm in Recovery from Western Civilization*. Boston and London: Shambhala.

Goffman, E (1997) *The Goffman Reader*. Oxford: Blackwell.

Gordon, P (2011) 'What do you do when you don't know what to do?' The respected other of Peter Lomas. *European Journal of Psychotherapy & Counselling, 13*(1), 23–32.

Gray, C (1988) *Leaving the Twentieth Century: The incomplete work of the Situationist International*. London: Rebel Press. (Original work published 1974)

Griggs, B (1982) *Green Pharmacy: A history of herbal medicine*. London: Jill Norman and Hobhouse.

Guattari, F (1984) *Molecular Revolution: Psychiatry and politics*. Harmondsworth: Penguin.

Gutheil, TG & Gabbard, GO (1993) The concept of boundaries in clinical practice: Theoretical and risk-management dimensions. *American Journal of Psychiatry, 150*, 188–96. Online at http://kspope.com/ethics/boundaries.php

Hall, GCN (2001) Psychotherapy research with ethnic minorities: Empirical, ethical, and conceptual issues. *Journal of Consulting and Clinical Psychology, 69*(3), 502–10.

Hardt, M & Negri, A (2006) *Multitude: War and democracy in the age of empire*. London: Penguin.

Hazan, C & Shaver, PR (1987) Romantic love conceptualized as an attachment process. *Journal of Personality and Social Psychology, 52*, 511–24.

Heaton, J (2011) The ordinary. *European Journal of Psychotherapy & Counselling, 13*(1), 47–55.

Heron, J (2011) The politics of transference. In R House & N Totton (Eds) *Implausible Professions: Arguments for pluralism and autonomy in psychotherapy and counselling* (2nd ed, pp 21–8). Ross-on-Wye: PCCS Books. (Original work published 1990)

Hillman, J & Ventura, M (1992) *We've Had 100 Years of Psychotherapy – and the World's Getting Worse*. San Francisco: HarperCollins.

Hinshelwood, RD (1997) *Therapy or Coercion?* London: Karnac.

Hogan, DB (1979) *The Regulation of Psychotherapists* (4 Vols). Cambridge, MA: Ballinger.

Hoggett, P (2004) Strange attractors: Politics and psychoanalysis. *Psychoanalysis, Culture and Society, 9,* 74–86.

Hollander, NC (2010) *Uprooted Minds: Surviving the politics of terror in the Americas*. Hove: Routledge.

House, R (1996) 'Audit-mindedness' in counselling: Some underlying dynamics. *British Journal of Guidance and Counselling, 24*(2), 277–83.

House, R (2011) Training: A guarantee of competence? In R House & N Totton (Eds) *Implausible Professions: Arguments for pluralism and autonomy in psychotherapy and counselling* (2nd ed, pp 114–24). Ross-on-Wye: PCCS Books. (Original work published 1997)

Jacobs, M (2005) *The Presenting Past: The core of psychodynamic counselling and therapy*. Maidenhead: Open University Press.

Jacoby, M (1986) Getting in touch and touching. In N Schwarz-Salant & M Stein (Eds) *The Body in Analysis* (pp 109–26). Wilmette, IL: Chiron.

Jacoby, R (1977) *Social Amnesia: A critique of conformist psychology from Adler to Laing*. Sussex: Harvester.

Jacoby, R (1986) *The Repression of Psychoanalysis: Otto Fenichel and the political Freudians*. Chicago: University of Chicago Press.

Jimenez, JP (1989) Some reflections on the practice of psychoanalysis in Chile today – From the point of view of the relationship between psychoanalysis and society. *International Review of Psycho-Analysis, 16,* 493–504.

Johnson, DH (Ed) (1997) *Groundworks: Narratives of embodiment*. Berkeley, CA: North Atlantic Books.

Johnson, S (2001a) Family therapy saves the planet: Messianic tendencies in family systems literature. *Journal of Marital and Family Therapy, 27,* 3–11.

Johnson, S (2001b) Saving the planet – or ourselves! *Journal of Marital and Family Therapy, 27,* 23–5.

Johnston, SH & Farber, BA (1996) The maintenance of boundaries in psychotherapeutic practice. *Psychotherapy, 33,* 391–402.

Jordan, JV (1995) A relational approach to psychotherapy. *Women & Therapy, 16*(4), 51–61.

Jordan, JV, Kaplan, AG, Miller, JB, Surrey, JL & Stiver, IP (1991) *Women's Growth in Connection: Writings from the Stone Center*. New York: Guilford Press.

Jung, CG (1976) *Letters, Vol II, 1951–61* (G Adler, Ed). London: Routledge and Kegan Paul.

Kearney, A (1996) *Counselling, Class and Politics*. Ross-on-Wye: PCCS Books.

Klein, M (1975) *Envy and Gratitude and Other Works*. New York: Delta.

Knight, RP (1953) The present status of organized psychoanalysis in the United States. *Journal of the American Psychoanalytic Association, 1*, 197–227.

Kobayashi, J (1989) Depathologizing dependency: Two perspectives. *Psychiatric Annals, 19*, 131–6.

Lago, C & Haugh, S (2006) White counsellor racial identity: The unacknowledged, unknown, unaware aspect of self in relationship. In G Proctor, M Cooper, P Sanders & B Malcolm (Eds) *Politicizing the Person-Centred Approach: An agenda for social change* (pp 198–214). Ross-on-Wye: PCCS Books.

Laing RD (1967) *The Politics of Experience and the Bird of Paradise*. Harmondsworth: Penguin.

Langs, R (1998) *Ground Rules in Psychotherapy and Counseling*. London: Karnac.

Larkin, G (1983) *Occupational Monopoly and Modern Medicine*. London: Tavistock.

Larson, M (1977) *The Rise of Professionalism*. Berkeley, CA: University of California Press.

Layton, L (2004) A fork in the royal road: On defining the unconscious and its stakes for social theory. *Psychoanalysis, Culture and Society, 9*(1), 33–51.

Layton, L (2006) Attacks on linking: The unconscious pull to dissociate individuals from their social context. In L Layton, NC Hollander & S Gutwill (Eds) *Psychoanalysis, Class and Politics: Encounters in the clinical setting* (pp 107–17). Hove: Routledge.

Lazarus, AA (1994) How certain boundaries and ethics diminish therapeutic effectiveness. *Ethics and Behavior, 4*(3), 255–61.

LeGuin, UK (1988) *Always Coming Home*. London: Grafton Books.

Levi-Strauss, C (1967) *Structural Anthropology*. New York: Anchor Books.

Little, M (1990) *Psychotic Anxieties and Containment: A personal record of an analysis with Winnicott*. Northvale, NJ: Jason Aronson.

Logan, S (2011) Peter Lomas's natural psychotherapy. *European Journal of Psychotherapy & Counselling, 13*(1), 33–46.

Lohser, B & Newton, PM (1996) *Unorthodox Freud: The view from the couch*. New York: Guilford Press.

Lomas, P (1987) *The Limits of Interpretation*. Harmondsworth: Penguin.

Lomas, P (1994) *True and False Experience: The human element in psychotherapy*. Piscataway, NJ: Transaction Publishers. (Original work published 1974)

Lomas, P (1994) *Cultivating Intuition: An introduction to psychotherapy*. London: Penguin.

Lomas, P (1999) *Doing Good? Psychotherapy out of its depth*. Oxford: Oxford University Press.

Lomas P (2011) The teaching of psychotherapy. In R House & N Totton (Eds) *Implausible Professions: Arguments for pluralism and autonomy in psychotherapy and counselling* (2nd ed, pp 238–47). Ross-on-Wye: PCCS Books. (Original work published 1997)

Lyon, MJ & Barbalet, JM (1994) Society's body. In TJ Csordas (Ed) *Embodiment and Experience* (pp 48–66). Cambridge: Cambridge University Press.

Macy, J (1991) *World as lover, world as self*. Berkeley, CA: Parallax Press.

Macy, J & Brown, M (1998) *Coming Back to Life: Practices to reconnect our lives, our world*. Gabriola Island, **BC**: New Society Publishers.

Mair, K (1992) The myth of therapist expertise. In W Dryden & C Feltham (Eds) *Psychotherapy and Its Discontents* (pp 135–68). Buckingham: Open University Press.

Mann, D (1997) *Psychotherapy: An erotic relationship. Transference and countertransference passions.* London: Routledge.

Marquis, JM (1972) An expedient model for behavior therapy. In AA Lazarus (Ed) *Clinical Behavior Therapy* (pp 41–72). New York: Brunner-Mazel.

Masson, J (Ed) (1985) *The Complete Letters of Sigmund Freud to Wilhelm Fliess, 1887–1904.* Cambridge, MA: Belknap Press.

Masson, J (1990) *Against Therapy.* London: Fontana.

McWhorter, J (Ed) (2000) *Language Change and Language Contact in Pidgins and Creoles.* Amsterdam: John Benjamins.

Mearns, D & Thorne, B (1988) *Person-Centred Counselling in Action.* London: Sage.

Meltzoff, AN & Moore, MK (1995) Infants' understanding of people and things: From body imitation to folk psychology. In JL Bermudez, A Marcel & N Eilan (Eds) *The Body and the Self* (pp 43–69). Cambridge MA: MIT Press.

Messler Davies, J (2004) Whose bad objects are we anyway? Repetition and our elusive love affair with evil. *Psychoanalytic Dialogues, 14*(6), 711–32.

Mindell, A (1985) *River's Edge: The process science of the dreambody.* London: Arkana.

Mindell, A (1988) *City Shadows: Psychological interventions in psychiatry.* London: Arkana.

Mindell, A (1992) *The Leader as Martial Artist: An introduction to deep democracy.* San Francisco: Harper.

Mindell, A (1995) *Sitting in the Fire: Large group transformation using conflict and diversity.* Portland, OR: Lao Tse Press.

Mindell, A & Mindell, A (1992) *Riding the Horse Backwards: Process work in theory and practice.* Harmondsworth: Penguin Arkana.

Morgan, S (2011) Peter and the renegade 'It was Georgie I loved best'. *European Journal of Psychotherapy & Counselling, 13*(1), 11–21.

Morgenthaler, F & Parin, P (1964) Typical forms of transference among West Africans. *International Journal of Psycho-Analysis, 45,* 446–9.

Mowbray, R (1995) *The Case against Psychotherapy Registration: A conservation issue for the Human Potential Movement.* London: Trans Marginal Press.

Newman, M (2010) Stark facts exposed about anti-regulation therapist. *Times Higher Education Supplement*, 28 January 2010. Online together with readers' responses at http://www.timeshighereducation.co.uk/story.asp?storycode=410179

Noel, B & Watterson, K (1992) *You Must Be Dreaming.* New York: Poseidon Press.

O'Hara, M (1997) Emancipatory therapeutic practice in a turbulent transmodern era: A work of retrieval. *Journal of Humanistic Psychology, 37*(3), 7–33.

Orbach, S (1998) *Fat is a Feminist Issue.* London: Arrow.

Orlinsky, DE & Howard, KI (1986) Process and outcome in psychotherapy. In SL Garfield & AE Bergin (Eds) *Handbook of Psychotherapy and Behavior Change* (pp 56–102). New York: Wiley.

Orwell, G (1946) Why I write. In *Why I write* (Penguin Great Ideas Series: pp. 1–10). London: Penguin. Online at http://homepage.mac.com/ericmacknight/Why_I_Write.pdf

Osborne, H (2006) Borrowers undaunted by debt. *The Guardian*, Wednesday April 19. Online at http://www.guardian.co.uk/business/2006/apr/19/creditanddebt.money?INTCMP=SRCH

Parkin, F (1974) Strategies of social closure in class formation. In F Parkin (Ed) *The Social Analysis of Class Structure* (pp 1–18). London: Tavistock.

Pearson, G (1983) *Hooligan: A history of respectable fears*. London: Macmillan.

Perls, F, Hefferline, RF & Goodman, P (1973) *Gestalt Therapy: Excitement and growth in the human personality*. Harmondsworth: Penguin. (Original work published 1951)

Perry, BD, Pollard, R, Blakley, TL, Baker, WL & Vigilante, D (1995) Childhood trauma, the neurobiology of adaptation, and 'use-dependent' development of the brain: How 'states' become 'traits'. *Infant Mental Health Journal, 16*(4), 271–91.

Phillips, A (1995) *Terrors and Experts*. London: Faber.

Pilgrim, D (1992) Psychotherapy and political evasions. In W Dryden & C Feltham (Eds) *Psychotherapy and its Discontents* (pp 225–43). Milton Keynes: Open University Press.

Pineda, JA (Ed) (2009) *Mirror Neuron Systems: The role of mirroring processes in social cognition*. New York: Humana Press.

Plant, S (1992) *The Most Radical Gesture: Situationist International in a postmodern age*. London: Routledge.

Polster, E & Polster, M (1974) *Gestalt Therapy Integrated: Contours of theory and practice*. New York: Vintage.

Poole, RW & Orski, CK (2000) HOT lanes: A better way to attack urban highway congestion. *Regulation, 23*(1), 15–20.

Porges, SW (1995) Orienting in a defensive world: Mammalian modifications of our evolutionary heritage. A polyvagal theory. *Psychophysiology, 32*, 301–318.

Porges, SW (1997) Emotion: An evolutionary by-product of the neural regulation of the autonomic nervous system. *Annals of the New York Academy of Sciences, 807*, 62–77.

Porges, SW (2005) The role of social engagement in attachment and bonding: A phylogenetic perspective. In CS Carter, L Ahnert, KE Grossmann, SB Hrdy, ME Lamb, SW Porges & N Sachser (Eds) *Attachment and Bonding: A new synthesis* (pp 33–54). Boston: MIT Press.

Poster, M (1978) *Critical Theory of the Family*. London: Pluto Press.

Postle, D (1998) The alchemist's nightmare: Gold into lead – The annexation of psychotherapy in the UK. *International Journal of Psychotherapy 3*(1), 53–83.

Postle, D (2011) Counselling in the UK: Jungle, garden or monoculture? In R House & N Totton (Eds) *Implausible Professions: Arguments for pluralism and autonomy in psychotherapy and counselling* (2nd ed, pp 170–78). Ross-on-Wye: PCCS Books. (Original work published 1997)

Powers, T (2004) Tomorrow the world. *New York Review of Books*, 11 March, 4–6.

Prescott, J (1975) Body pleasure and the origins of violence. *Bulletin of Atomic Scientists*, November, 10–20. Online at http://www.violence.de/prescott/bulletin/article.html

Proctor, G, Cooper, M, Sanders, P & Malcolm, B (Eds) (2006) *Politicizing the Person-Centred Approach: An agenda for social change*. Ross-on-Wye: PCCS Books.

Reich, W (1973) *The Function of the Orgasm*. London: Souvenir Press. (Original work published 1942)

Reich, W (1975) *The Mass Psychology of Fascism*. Harmondsworth: Penguin Books. (Original work published 1933)

Richards, S, Hargaden, H & Beazley Richards, J (1998) Letter. *Counselling*, 9(3), 173.

Rogers, CR (1978) *Carl Rogers on Personal Power: Inner strength and its revolutionary impact*. London: Constable.

Rogers, CR (1980) Some new challenges to the helping professions. In *A Way of Being* (pp 235–59). Boston: Houghton Mifflin. (Original work published 1973)

Rose, N (1990) *Governing the Soul: The shaping of the private self*. London: Routledge.

Roszak, T, Gomes, ME & Kanner, AD (Eds) (1995) *Ecopsychology; Restoring the earth, healing the mind*. San Francisco: Sierra Club Books.

Roth, A & Fonagy, P (1996) *What Works for Whom? A critical review of psychotherapy research*. London: Guilford Press.

Samuels, A (1993) *The Political Psyche*. London: Routledge.

Samuels, A (2001) *Politics on the Couch: Citizenship and the internal life*. London: Profile Books.

Samuels, A (2006) Working directly with political, cultural, and social material in the therapy session. In L Layton, NC Hollander & S Gutwill (Eds) *Psychoanalysis, Class and Politics: Encounters in the clinical setting* (pp 11–28). Hove: Routledge.

Samuels, A (2011) Pluralism and psychotherapy: What is a good training? In R House & N Totton (Eds) *Implausible Professions: Arguments for pluralism and autonomy in psychotherapy and counselling* (2nd ed, pp 221–37). Ross-on-Wye: PCCS Books. (Original work published 1997)

Sandler, J (1983) Reflections on some relations between psychoanalytic concepts and psychoanalytic practice. *International Journal of Psycho-Analysis*, 64, 35–45.

Sands, A (2000) *Falling for Therapy: Psychotherapy from a client's point of view*. London: Palgrave Macmillan.

Saunders, S (1998) Envy, elitism and egoism: Whose interests are counsellors meeting? *Counselling*, 9(3), 179–80.

Schore, AN (2000) The effects of early relational trauma on right brain development, affect regulation, and infant mental health. *Infant Mental Health Journal*, 22(1–2), 201–69.

Seager, A (2006) Homes crisis feared as households projected to rise by nearly a quarter. *The Guardian*, Wednesday March 15. Online at http://www.guardian.co.uk/money/2006/mar/15/business.communities?INTCMP=SRCH

References 173

Segal, H (1988) Silence is the real crime. In JB Levine, D Jacobs & LJ Rubin (Eds) *Psychoanalysis and the Nuclear Threat: Clinical and theoretical studies* (pp 35–8). Hillsdale, NJ: Analytic Press.

Seidler, VJ (2010) Cultural memory and psychosocial narratives: Remembering 1968. *Psychotherapy and Politics International, 8*(3), 181–97.

Seligman, MEP (1995) The effectiveness of psychotherapy: The Consumer Reports study. *American Psychologist, 50*(12), 965–74.

Sharaf, M (1983) *Fury on Earth*. London: Hutchinson.

Shilling, C (1993) *The Body and Social Theory*. London: Sage.

Shiva, V (1993). *Monocultures of the Mind: Perspectives on biodiversity and biotechnology*. London: Zed Books.

Simon, RI (1989) Sexual exploitation of patients: How it begins before it happens. *Psychiatric Annals, 19*, 104–22.

Smith, DL (1991) Maintaining boundaries in psychotherapy: A view from evolutionary psychoanalysis. In C Feltham (Ed) *Controversies in Psychotherapy and Counselling* (pp 132–41). London: Sage.

Solomon, M (1994) *Lean on Me: The power of positive dependency in intimate relationships*. Riverside, NJ: Simon and Schuster.

Spinelli, E (1998) Interview: Counselling and the abuse of power. *Counselling, 9*(3), 181–4.

Spinelli, E (2002) *The Mirror and the Hammer: Challenging orthodoxies in psychotherapeutic thought*. London: Sage.

Stacey, M (1992) *Regulating Medicine: The General Medical Council*. London: Wiley.

Stacey, M (1994) Collective therapeutic responsibility: Lessons from the GMC. In S Budd & U Sharma (Eds) *The Healing Bond: The patient–practitioner relationship and therapeutic responsibility* (pp 107–133). London: Routledge.

Stehr, N (1994) *Knowledge Societies*. London: Sage.

Steiner, CM (1981) *The Other Side of Power*. New York: Grove Press. Revised edition online at http://www.claudesteiner.com/osp.htm

Stern, D (1985) *The Interpersonal World of the Infant*. New York: Basic Books.

Stone, H & Stone, S (2004) An open letter to the President. *Psychotherapy and Politics International, 2*(1), 64–9.

Suzuki, S (1973) *Zen Mind, Beginner's Mind*. New York: Weatherhill.

Sweetman, P (1999) Anchoring the (postmodern) self? Body modification, fashion and identity. *Body and Society, 5*, 51–76.

Tantam, D & van Deurzen, E (1998) Creating a European profession of psychotherapy. *European Journal of Psychotherapy, Counselling and Health, 1*(1), 121–35.

Thorne, B (1987) Beyond the core conditions. In W Dryden (Ed) *Key Cases in Psychotherapy* (pp 48–77). London: Croom Helm.

Thorne, B (2011) The accountable therapist: Standards, experts and poisoning the well. In R House & N Totton (Eds) *Implausible Professions: Arguments for pluralism and autonomy in psychotherapy and counselling* (2nd ed, pp 161–9). Ross-on-Wye: PCCS Books. (Original work published 1995)

Totton, N (1998a) The Independent Practitioners Network: A new model of accountability. *Dialogue, 1*(1), 30–3.

Totton, N (1998b) *The Water in the Glass: Body and mind in psychoanalysis*. London: Karnac/Rebus Press.
Totton, N (1999) The baby and the bathwater: 'Professionalisation' in psychotherapy and counselling. *British Journal of Guidance and Counselling, 27*(3), 313–24.
Totton, N (2000) *Psychotherapy and Politics*. London: Sage.
Totton, N (2003) The ecological self: Introducing ecopsychology. *CPJ, 14*(9), 14–18.
Totton, N (2005) Can psychotherapy help make a better future? *Psychotherapy and Politics International, 3*(2), 83–95.
Totton, N (2006a) Power in the therapeutic relationship. In N Totton (Ed) *The Politics of Psychotherapy: New perspectives* (pp 83–93). Maidenhead: Open University Press.
Totton, N (Ed) (2006b) *The Politics of Psychotherapy: New perspectives*. Maidenhead: Open University Press.
Totton, N (2006c) The institutions of psychotherapy. In N Totton (Ed) *The Politics of Psychotherapy: New perspectives* (pp 108–20). Maidenhead: Open University Press.
Totton, N (2006d) Introduction. In N Totton (Ed) *The Politics of Psychotherapy: New Perspectives* (pp xiii–xx). Maidenhead: Open University Press.
Totton, N (2006e) Birth, death, orgasm and perversion: A Reichian view. In D Nobus & L Downing (Eds) *Perversion: Psychoanalytic perspectives/ perspectives on psychoanalysis* (pp. 127–146). London: Karnac.
Totton, N (2008) Being, having, and becoming bodies. *Body, Movement and Dance in Psychotherapy, 5*(1), 21–30.
Totton, N (2011a) Inputs and outcomes: The medical model and professionalisation. In R House & N Totton (Eds) *Implausible Professions: Arguments for pluralism and autonomy in psychotherapy and counselling* (2nd ed, pp 125–32). Ross-on-Wye: PCCS Books. (Original work published 1997).
Totton, N (2011b) Learning by mistake: Client–practitioner conflicts in a self-regulated network. In R House & N Totton (Eds) *Implausible Professions: Arguments for pluralism and autonomy in psychotherapy and counselling* (2nd ed, pp 342–8). Ross-on-Wye: PCCS Books. (Original work published 1997)
Totton, N (2011c) *Wild Therapy: Undomesticating inner and outer worlds*. Ross-on-Wye: PCCS Books.
Totton, N (2012) 'Nothing's out of order': Towards an ecological therapy. In M-J Rust & N Totton *Vital Signs: Psychological responses to ecological crisis* (pp. 253–64). London: Karnac.
Totton, N & Edmondson, E (2009) *Reichian Growth Work: Melting the blocks to life and love* (2nd ed). Ross-on-Wye: PCCS Books.
Trevarthen, C & Aitken, KJ (2001) Infant intersubjectivity: Research, theory and clinical applications. *Journal of Child Psychology and Psychiatry, 42*(1), 3–48.
Van der Ploeg, JD (1993) Potatoes and knowledge. In M Hobart (Ed) *An Anthropological Critique of Development: The growth of ignorance* (pp 209–27). London: Routledge.

References 175

Van Deurzen, E (1996) *Registration: What it will mean to you as a counsellor*. 5th St Georges Counselling in Primary Care Conference, Keynote Address.

Vidal, J (2005). Rainforest loss shocks Brazil. *The Guardian*, Friday 20 May. Online at http://www.guardian.co.uk/news/2005/may/20/brazil.environment?INTCMP=SRCH

Wasdell, D (2011) In the shadow of accreditation. In R House & N Totton (Eds) *Implausible Professions: Arguments for pluralism and autonomy in psychotherapy and counselling* (2nd ed, pp 29-42). Ross-on-Wye: PCCS Books. (Original work published 1992)

Weiss, AG (2002) The lost role of dependency in psychotherapy. *Gestalt Review*, 6(1), 6-17.

West, W (1988) *Melting Armour*. Self-published, available from 12 Torbay Rd, Manchester M212 8XD, UK.

Winnicott, DW (1987) Hate in the countertransference. In *Through Paediatrics to Psychoanalysis: Collected Papers* (pp 194-203). London: Karnac Books. (Original work published 1947)

Winnicott, DW (1992) Mind and its relation to the psyche-soma. In *Through Paediatrics to Psychoanalysis: Collected Papers* (pp 243-54). London: Karnac Books. (Original work published 1949)

Wyckoff, H (Ed) (1976) *Love, Therapy and Politics*. New York: Grove Press.

Wynne, B (1995) May the sheep safely graze? A reflexive view of the expert-lay knowledge divide. In S Lash, B Szerzynzki & B Wynne (Eds) *Risk, Environment and Modernity: Towards a new ecology* (pp 44-83). London: Sage.

Younge, G (2003) Shades of grey. Interview with Hans Blix. Guardian, March 28th. Online at http://www.guardian.co.uk/world/2003/mar/28/iraq.garyyounge

Zur, O (2004) To cross or not to cross: Do boundaries in therapy protect or harm? *Psychotherapy Bulletin, 39*(3), 27-32.

Index

A
abuse 65, 103ff, 124, 150, 156
  by practitioners 5, 12f, 20, 23, 44, 124, 146
Alliance for Counselling and Psychotherapy 22–3, 26
amae 41
anarchism vii, x
anxiety 13, 30, 55, 71, 74, 77, 80, 102, 142, 153
apologising to clients 12, 18, 32, 37, 108
Aslan 70–1
attachment 42, 143, 148, 155, 163
authority 29, 41, 116, 120–1, 126, 148
autonomic nervous system 143ff

B
babies 13, 42, 45, 141, 143, 148, 157–8
BACP (British Association for Counselling and Psychotherapy) 17, 33, 44, 71, 96, 112, 141
'big P' politics 31, 94–5
  (See also macropolitics, 'small p' politics)
biosphere 43, 58, 105
black clients 119, 123
black therapists 121
bodies 5, 24, 47ff, 73f, 141–2, 148–9, 155, 157ff
body psychotherapy 17, 42, 74, 76, 141–2, 145, 148–9, 157–61, 163
bond, social 11, 42, 79, 104, 143, 148, 157, 163
boundaries 8, 11, 13, 26, Ch 11 passim, 80, 146–7
boundlessness 70
breath, breathing 49, 69, 76, 144, 159
brief therapy 39, 125
  (See also solution-focused therapy)
Bush, George W 94, 103, 110, 113–14

C
capitalism 11, 13–14, 100, 104, 120, 128, 150, 155, 156
CCTV 20, 45, 68, 136
Chile 117
citizenship 86, 114, 136
class, classism 32, 116, 118, 120–2
climate change 108, 111, 150–1, 156
Cognitive Behavioural Therapy (CBT) 60, 61, 66, 73
communication styles 122–3
complaints 12, 18, 44, 128
complexity 15, 24, 152, 154, 156
  and overwhelm 150
  of psyche 61
  of society 80
  of therapeutic contexts 115, 126
  of therapeutic explanations 123
conflict resolution 12, 17–18, 89, 94, 101–3, 111, 163
consciousness 66, 72, 76, 86, 154–6
conservativism 57, 87, 93, 98, 119
consistency, requirement for 48, 73–7
contact, psychological 42, 66, 69, 105, 145–9, 155, 157
control
  of therapy/therapists 8, 11–12, 14–15, 22–6, 63, 64, 72, 153

of language 57
of self 71–2, 97, 142, 147, 149, 152, 153
of society 25, 26, 64, 72, 80, 84, 86, 110–11, 138, 155
of the world/nature 105, 152–4
(See also power)
countertransference 46, 75, 160–3
(See also transference)
creole 36, 107
(See also pidgin)
cure, therapeutic goal of 92, 94, 96–7, 99, 117, 124

D
Davies, Jody Messler 68–9
defensive practice 25, 45, 67, 71, 155
(See also undefensive practice)
democracy 120
  'deep democracy' 35, 61, 111, 113–14
  inner 113–14
  and therapy Ch 17 passim
dependency in therapy 30, 34, Ch 7 passim, 124–5, 141–2, 147, 152, 154, 157–8
(See also interdependence)
dependent co-arising 152
despair and empowerment work 106
(See also Macy, Joanna)
difference
  tolerating 25, 62, 113, 115, 119–20
  of rank 32, 120ff
  between therapists Ch 6 passim, 60ff
disclosure in therapy 57
disembodiment 157–8
(See also dissociation)
dissociation 49, 88, 94, 103–5, 115, 116, 143, 151, 155
Dogon tribe 126
domestication 58, 64, 72, 80, 153–4
Diagnostic and Statistical Manual, 4th edition (*DSM-IV*) 7
dualism 6, 26, 86, 103ff, 127

E
ecology, ecosystems 58, 152, 155
  deep, 111
  of therapy 24, 33
ecological
  crisis 94, 105, 111, 150, 152
  /ecosystemic thinking ix, 152, 153, 155
economics 4, 20, 25, 34, 39, 41, 88, 124–5, 156
ecopsychology ix, 89, 101, 103–5, Ch 22 passim, Ch 23 passim
Embodied-Relational Therapy (ERT) 141, 147
embodiment 34, 38, 42, 48–50, 69, 79, Ch 21 passim, 154, 155, Ch 24 passim
enactment, re-enactment 31–2, 37, 103–6, 119, 160
enlightenment practice, therapy as 75
erotic charge 48–50
European Association for Body Psychotherapy (EABP) 157
evidence-based practice 23, 25, 26, 51, 63, 136
exaptation 144, 148
expertise, expert systems 3, 8–12, 15–16, 29, 33–4, 36, 37, 40, 66, 77–80, 86, 95, 98–101, 107, 113, 116, 122, 125, 148
(See also local knowledge/s)

F
False Memory Syndrome 124
families 34, 40, 74–5, 91, 92, 94–5, 104, 116, 122, 123, 137
fear 36, 38, 42, 124, 146ff, 153
  of clients 13, 67
  of dependency 38, 42, 124
  of relationship 142, 146–7
  of therapist 36, 124
  of the uncontrollable 142, 153
Ferenczi, Sandor 49, 76
Foucault, Michel 14, 93, 138
free association 47–8, 76
Freud, Sigmund 3, 6, 7, 37, 47, 64, 65–6, 71, 88, 93, 104

G

gender 41, 74, 89, 120, 122, 158
  issues in therapy 118ff
generic therapy 8–11, 59, 60
goals, therapeutic vii, 23–4, 34–5, 72–3, 77, 86–7, 93, 97, 117, 128
Gordon, Paul 52, 58
'growers' club' 33

H

Health Professions Council (HPC) 19, 22–6, 111, 178
Heaton, John 52–6
helping, role of in therapy 25, 31, Ch 6 passim, 71, 76, 85, 136, 149, 153, 158
history of therapy viii-ix
human nature 14, 86, 87, 132, 136, 155
humanistic therapy 30, 52, 54, 60, 66, 89, 129, 134–5

I

Independent Practitioners Network (IPN) 14, 17–19
individual vs group paradigm ix
infancy 41, 126, 137, 141–4, 148, 157
infantilisation 94, 126
insurance 7, 40, 77
interdependence 41, 42–3, 154
internal critic 67, 73, 105
interpellation 74–5, 77, 138
intimacy 40, Ch 8 passim, 53, 127, 141, 148, 161
intuition 10, 16, 34, 53, 56, 136
Iraq 39, 91, 94, 113, 116, 118

J

Jung, Carl 3, 10
jungle 154
  (See also rainforest)

K

'Ken' (client) 161ff

L

language/s in therapy 36–7, 50, 52–6, 107–8
  (See also creole, pidgin)
Layton, Lynne 74, 119
LeGuin, Ursula 153
local knowledge/s 8–11, 14, 16, 33–6, 77–9, 99–100
  (See also expertise, expert systems)
Logan, Stephen 52, 58
Lomas, Peter 4, 10, 16, Ch 9 passim, 64
LSD 134

M

macropolitics 91–2
  (See also micropolitics, 'big P' politics)
Macy, Joanna ix, 106
mainstream, cultural/political 41, 91, 115, 119–22, 129, 135, 159
mammalian neurology 144, 151
managed care 7, 11, 100, 125
Marx, Karl 96, 137
Maugrim 72, 80
May '68 Ch 19 passim, 131, 133
medical model in therapy 3, 7, 8–9, 19, 23–5, 78, 117, 121, 126
micropolitics 91–2, 94–5, 137
  (See also macropolitics, 'small p' politics)
middle class 120–2
Mindell, Amy 97
Mindell, Arnold 33, 44, 61, 97, 111, 113–14, 119–22
minority cultures 41, 120
  (See also non-mainstream cultures)
mirror neurones 143
modalities, therapeutic 23, 25, 60–1
monitoring 15, 25, 45, 67, 72, 81, 153
  (See also surveillance)
Morgan, Sian 52, 53, 55, 58–9
mothering 42, 77, 91, 126, 141, 143, 144, 148
  (See also parenting)

N

'Naomi' (client) 160ff
National Health Service (NHS) 7, 8, 124–6
negotiating 32, 35–6, 62, 67, 89, 93, 94, 102–3, 108, 113–14, 125, 163
neuroscience 20, 103, 142–8
neutrality, therapeutic, myth of 60, 67, 87, 93, 118, 119, 163
non-mainstream cultures 120, 122, 159
(See also minority cultures)
'normality' 6–7, 77–8, 97
normative unconscious (Lynne Layton) 74, 119

O

Occupy movement vii, 26
ordinariness 12, 34, 44, Ch 9 passim, 94, 100, 104, 142
other-than-human 58, 153–4, 156, 158, 163
outcome research 8, 11, 33, 60–1, 77, 125
overwhelm 146, Ch 22 passim, 156, 161
oxytocin 148

P

paradox 35, 52–4, 73–6, 138, 142, 152
parenting 37, 41, 45, 46–7, 50, 55, 108
(See also mothering)
paticca samuppada 152
patriarchy 104, 131, 155
pidgin 36, 107
(See also creole)
pluralism 16, 35, Ch 10 passim, 89, 99, 108, 114
political energy 94–5, 116, 129
politicians 88–9, 108
'politics on the couch' 88
Polyvagal Theory 143ff
Porges, Stephen 143ff, 148
Postle, Denis 11, 13, 19, 61

power passim
  in the therapy room Ch 5 passim, 32, 36, 37, 39, 50, 57, 87, 90–1, 106–8, 112–13, 119, 121, 125, 137, 142, 153, 156, 158
professionalisation of therapy Ch 1 passim, 23, 78, 99–100, 135
projection 12–13, 66
  and politics 88, 101–3, 114, 138
prostitution, therapy as 47, 124
psychoanalysis 3, 6, 7, 17, 46, 51, 52, 54–5, 63, 65, 77, 100, 117–18, 126–7, 134
(See also Freud)
Psychotherapy and Politics International Ch 14 passim, 91, 128

R

racism 32, 57, 88, 89, 91, 94, 102
rainforest 15ff
  therapy as viii, 19, 61
(See also jungle)
rank 8, 32, 78, 119–22
récupération 128
regulation of therapy and counselling xi, Part 1 passim, 135, 153
Reich, Wilhelm 6, 72, 100, 116, 128, 134, 137
relationship, therapeutic 7, 9, 11, 16–17, 23–5, Ch 5 passim, 36, 39, 45–6, 48–50, 51, 53–4, 57, 60, 63, 64, 66, 68–70, 80, 90, 106–8, 113, Ch 18 passim, 145, 147, 148–9, 160–63
relaxation
  and excitement x
  role of in therapy 42, 70, 71, 77, 142, 144, 147, 148, 149
reparation, therapeutic 31, 46, 75, 148
revolution 21, 94, 128, 130, 133–5
risk, inherent to therapy x, 25, 67, 69, 136
Rogers, Carl 3, 72, 116, 129, 137

S

Samuels, Andrew 22, 61–2, 88, 91, 94–5, 99, 106, 116, 129, 155
scapegoating 13, 74, 88
Seidler, Victor Jeneliewski 130–1
sexism 32, 88–9, 91, 94, 102, 131
sexual orientation 119, 162
sexuality 46–7, 49, 89, 97, 120, 122, 124, 128, 162–3
shadow, the 13, 41, 88
'slippery slope' theory 65
'small p' politics 54, 94–5
   (See also micropolitics, 'big P' politics)
Social Engagement System 145, 148
social responsibility 91, 94
solution-focused therapy 39, 125
'spastic ego' 77
speciation 33
Spinelli, Ernesto 5, 16
spontaneity 30, 47–8, 50, 63–4, 74–6, 93, 97, 117, 149, 152, 154
subjectivity 69, 86, 137, 138, 148
surveillance 15, 26, 72, 81, 128, 136, 153
   (See also monitoring)

T

Tao Te Ching 153
The Politics of Psychotherapy Ch 20 passim
Therapy Police 44–5, 63, 68, 80
Thorne, Brian 4, 8, 12–13, 64, 112
Totschweigen 4
touch in therapy 64, 149, 163
training of counsellors and psychotherapists 4–8, 11, 17, 24–5, 50, 60, 63–4, 77–9, 80, 99, 118, 121, 122, 126
transference 45–6, 50, 66, 75, 118
   child-to-child, 45
   (See also countertransference)
trauma 31, 37, 55, 86, 101, 103–6, 108, 130, 146, 150, 155, 157–8
   societal 103–6, 155–6
truth ix–x, 3, 35, 37, 89, 95, 108, 116

U

United Kingdom Council for Psychotherapy (UKCP) 8, 9, 11, 13, 17, 19, 22, 112
unconscious
   motivations and attitudes 14, 30–2, 64, 92–3, 96–9, 109, 115, 121, 135, 138, 142
   the, 15, 72, 138, 142
   (See also normative unconscious)
undefensive practice 67, 69, 70, 155
   (See also defensive practice)

V

van der Ploeg, Jan 9, 16, 79
voluntary sector 24, 125–6

W

whites 41, 120–3
'White Witch' 72, 80
Wild Therapy Ch 23 passim
Wild Therapy (2011) vii–viii, 58, 63, 152, 154, 155
Winnicott, DW 13, 64, 72, 77, 143
working class 116, 118
Wynne, Brian 9–10, 16

Wild Therapy: Undomesticating inner and outer worlds
Nick Totton

ISBN 978 1 906254 36 0
£16.99 rrp / £16.00 direct

Therapy is by nature wild; but a lot of it at the moment is rather tame. This book tries to shift the balance back towards wildness, by connecting therapy with ecological thinking, seeing each species, each being, and each person inherently and profoundly linked to each other.

> Nick Totton's 'Wild Therapy' is a call from nature to rediscover the earth and relationship to the universe. Totton's 'wildness' is a breath of fresh air, freeing therapies and cultures to live closer to the Tao. Read, dream, and be moved by his book!
> Arnold Mindell, author of *Processmind*

Reichian Growth Work: Melting the blocks to life and love
Nick Totton & Em Edmondson

ISBN 978 1 906254 12 4
£12.99 rrp / £12.00 direct

A revised and updated new edition of a body psychotherapy classic, *Reichian Growth Work* sets out to convey the essential features of Reichian therapy in concrete and easily understandable language. The style of body therapy which it describes is democratic, growth-oriented and undogmatic, while still committed to Reich's radical description of human beings and their difficulties. This book is for people who want to change; because only by changing, profoundly painful as that sometimes is, can we stay alive and growing.

> Maybe capitalism's latest crisis will force people to re-read Reich as the relevant theorist of alternative ways to organise our world. If that thought interests you, start here ...
> Andrew Samuels, Professor of Analytical Psychology, University of Essex

Implausible Professions: Arguments for pluralism and autonomy in psychotherapy and counselling 2nd extended edition
Richard House & Nick Totton, editors

ISBN 978 1 906254 33 9
£22.00 rrp / £20.00 direct

This edition contains a completely new Editorial, Introduction and Conclusion, updating the story to 2011. For those engaging with the politics of professionalisation for the first time, or wanting to refresh themselves about the reasons why counselling and psychotherapy are in principle 'implausible professions', this text is even more indispensable than it was in 1997.

www.pccs-books.co.uk